D1528226

Native

American Bows

by T. M. Hamilton

Second Edition

With an Appendix
by Bill Holm
On Making Horn Bows.

Also

Photos of Horn Bows from the Collection

of

Charles E. Grayson

Missouri Archaeological Society
Columbia, Missouri
Special Publications No. 5
1982

To The Memory
of
Alfred Vincent Kidder
and
Remington Schuyler

"DEER HUNTING." How deer could be stalked before they had been alarmed by the gun. An engraving by De Bry after a lost painting by Le Moyne made between 1562 and 1565. *THE NEW WORLD, by Stefan Lorant.*

Table of Contents

Illustrations

Figure

Introduction To Second Edition

It has been ten years since the first edition of this book on the archery of the Natives of the Western hemisphere came off the press. I am surprised that more new information has not come to light during the intervening years, but I can find nothing which would justify drastic rewriting. However, I am pleased to acknowledge two authorities whose studies have complimented my own work and whose contributions have been added here.

Bill Holm, Curator of Northwest Coast Indian Art at the Thomas Burke Memorial Washington State Museum, Seattle, has made several successful bows from both mountain sheep horn and elk antler using the information to be found in Chapter 6, pages 94 to 96, which I published with the permission of the American Museum of Natural History.

I have been able to prevail upon Mr. Holm to write up in detail exactly how he made the horn bows, and his description of the processes, along with his excellent photographs, have been added as an Appendix.

Charles (Bert) Grayson of Clatskanie, Oregon, is another authority on archery with a world wide reputation, and I have been gratified with the interest he has taken in the original edition and its proposed republication. He has reread the first edition carefully with this in mind and has given it his approval with a few minor reservations. His only serious criticism is my labeling the 35 inch elkhorn bow (Figure 32) a boy's bow. It is his opinion that this was a man's bow made to do a man's work, and that Catlin's remarks about the performance of the extremely short "bone" bows was correct and factual. This is also Mr. Holm's opinion and I defer to their judgement. They do agree with me though that Catlin was in error in thinking that these bows were made from a bone of a whale; that they were actually made either from elk antler or mountain sheep horn and *always* backed with sinew.

Dr. Grayson has also furnished photographs of choice specimens of the horn bow in his collection and I am grateful for his permission to include them in the Appendix.

When this book was first being written, beginning some twenty-five years ago, the plastic bow was in the process of supplanting the old traditional long or flat bows. Since then, the plastic bow has been supplanted by the new compound bow with its array of pulleys and string, and few "archers" would be caught out in the light of day with an old fashioned bow which he had made himself. Fashions come and go, and it is my sincere hope that this book will arouse the curiosity of future generations in the traditional bows, and an appreciation of their simple beauty in action; and that these new archers realize the tremendous satisfaction to be had in shooting and hunting with tackle which one has made himself.

For them we have assembled here all the basic information we have been able to rescue from oblivion. Bill Holm, Bert Grayson and I wish them good shooting.

Miami, Missouri   T. M. Hamilton
65344

Acknowledgments

Dr. Carl H. Chapman, professor of anthropology and Director of Archaeological Research Activities, University of Missouri, first suggested that I undertake this study when I complained to him about the inadequacies of bow descriptions found in the various journals of his profession.

Dr. A.V. Kidder of Peabody Museum, Harvard University, was most enthusiastic about my proposed study when I wrote him for information on the various bows at that institution. He not only had them photographed, but continued to take an active interest in my work until shortly before his death. Without his personal sponsorship certain important sources of information would not have been made available to me.

The late Remington Schuyler, a nephew of Frederick Remington and a Western artist in his own right, left me his collection of native American bows which, added to the few I had, have been invaluable for reference purposes. Mr. Schuyler also described in detail his observances of Indian shooting and bow handling during his years spent as a trader on the Rosebud Reservation at the turn of the century.

Dr. Robert F.G. Spier, University of Missouri; Dr. Clifford Evans and Dr. Betty Meggers of the Smithsonian Institution; Dr. Frank Leonhardy, then of the Museum of the Great Plains, and Col. Wilbur Burgess of Fort Sill all read preliminary drafts and wrote detailed and valuable criticisms which have definitely helped in the presentation of my findings and conclusions.

Dr. Albert H. Schroeder of the National Park Service brought to my attention the problem of the "Turkish" bows, reported by the early Spanish explorers, and furnished the citations on the question as discussed in Chapter IV.

Lt. Cdr. W.F. Paterson of Hants, England, and Edwin McEwen of London, both of the Society of Archer Antiquaries, have been extremely patient in explaining to me the esoteric details of the Asiatic composite, and Mr. McEwen presented me with a Turkish bow, complete with both flight and war arrows, so I could gain first-hand experience with the weapon.

Thomas D. Napier of Seoul, Korea, likewise obtained three Korean composites for me, complete with arrows, quivers and a thumb ring which fits!

Alan R. Woolworth of the Minnesota Historical Society; Dr. Dale Henning, now of the University of Nebraska, and Harold L. Peterson, chief curator of the National Park Service, have all kept my research in mind through the years and have each sent me many references found where I never would have had the opportunity to look.

The quotations from Alfred Jacob Miller and the two reproductions of his watercolors are taken by special permission from THE WEST OF ALFRED JACOB

MILLER, by Alfred Jacob Miller, with an account of the artist by Marvin C. Ross. (Copyright 1951, 1968, University of Oklahoma Press.)

The quotation from Garcilaso is from THE FLORIDA OF THE INCA, translated by John Grier Varner and Jeannette Johnson Varner, copyright 1951 by the University of Texas Press and published here by special permission.

The remarkable drawings of John White and De Bry's engravings after Le Moyne are from Stefan Lorant's THE NEW WORLD (Meredith, copyright 1946). They are reproduced here through the cooperation of Mr. Lorant.

I am indebted to the American Museum of Natural History, New York, for abstracting Wolf-chief's account of the making of the horn bow from the field notes made by Dr. Gilbert L. Wilson when working among the Hidatsa in 1910, and for their permission to incorporate that information into the chapter on the American composite. Until such time as the Museum publishes Dr. Wilson's notes on the horn bow in their entirety, including his sketches and those by Wolf-chief, this abstract will stand as the most complete and detailed description of the process available.

The basic research in native archery was done some fifty years ago by the late Dr. Saxton T. Pope and the Yahi Indian, Ishi. In my rather extensive library on archery the most prized items are the entire series of Dr. Pope's reports, inscribed in his hand to Remington Schuyler, and his correspondence with Mr. Schuyler. The two had much in common.

The arms historian, Harold L. Peterson of the National Park Service, has given me various leads and valued advice during the years. His availability has been greatly appreciated.

I consider myself fortunate in having Dr. George Shumway for my publisher. He has taken a personal interest in the work as it progressed and has made many excellent suggestions and criticisms. No less helpful has been my editor, Mrs. Nancy Bagby. It has been a pleasure to work with her, and her tact, wisdom and good judgment are freely acknowledged.

In looking through my notes I am astounded at the number of individuals who have been consulted during the seventeen years this study has been in progress. Where specific contributions are incorporated into the text, such as that of George Metcalf of the Smithsonian, the name of the individual is given, but it is only just that all who cooperated should also be recognized, individually and by name. I trust that there are none who have been overlooked inadvertently in the listing which follows. The locations given are as they were at the time of consultation.

E.R. Adair, Longview, Washington.

B.A. Bendtsen, National Wood Products Laboratory, Madison, Wisconsin.

Paul R. Brayton, Jr., The American Museum of Natural History.

Warren W. Caldwell, Smithsonian Institution, Lincoln, Nebraska.

Chester S. Chard, University of Wisconsin.

Harry and Hugh Collins, Sedalia, Missouri; archers and bowmakers.

Henry B. Collins, Smithsonian Institution.

Aaron J. Cosner, Globe, Arizona; archer and bowmaker.

G.F. Cresswell, Potosi, Missouri.

R.A. Elder, Jr., Assistant Curator, Division of Ethnology, Smithsonian Institution.

Albert B. Elsasser, Department of Anthropology, University of California.

John C. Ewers, U.S. National Museum, Washington.

George E. Fay, Colorado State College, Greeley, Colorado.

Franklin Fenenga, Department of Anthropology, University of Nebraska.

Stanley A. Freed, The American Museum of Natural History, New York City.

Phillip C. Gifford, The American Museum of Natural History, New York City.

Robert E. Greengo, The Peabody Museum, Cambridge, Massachusetts.

Henry W. Hamilton, Marshall, Missouri.

Dale Henning, University of Nebraska.

Adrian Eliot Hodgkin, Surrey, England; archer.

James H. Howard, Kansas City Museum, Kansas City, Missouri.

Al Hunter, Anadarko, Oklahoma; Indian and Indian style archer.

Diamond Jenness, Ottawa, Canada.

W.A. Kenyon, Toronto, Canada.

Marvin Kivett, State Historical Society Museum, Lincoln, Nebraska.

Robert C. Koeppen, Woods Products Laboratory, Madison, Wisconsin.

Reginald Laubin, Moose, Montana; Indian style archer.

Savoie Lottinville, Director, University of Oklahoma Press, Norman, Oklahoma.

T.M.N. Lewis, Tennessee Archaeological Society.

Richard S. Marshall, Department of Anthropology, University of Missouri.

Paul S. Martin, Chief Curator, Department of Anthropology, Chicago Museum of
    Natural History, Illinois.

George Metcalf, Aide, Division of Archaeology, Smithsonian Institution.

Charles Miles, Oakland, California.

Walter Perry, Bend, Oregon; archer.

Harold L. Peterson, National Park Service, Washington, D.C.

George Quimby, Curator of American Archaeology, Museum of Natural History, Chicago, Illinois.

Eugene Robinson, Napa, California.

H.L. Shapiro, Chairman of the Department of Anthropology, The American Museum of Natural History, New York City.

Leslie Spier, Editor, SOUTHWESTERN JOURNAL OF ANTHROPOLOGY, Albuquerque, New Mexico.

Charlie Steen, National Park Service, Santa Fe, New Mexico.

Vilhjalmur Stefansson, Dartmouth College.

Robert L. Stephenson, Smithsonian Institution, Lincoln, Nebraska.

Raymond S. Sullivan, Captain, U.S.Navy.

Marvin E. Tong, Jr., Director, Museum of the Great Plains, Lawton, Oklahoma.

Tom Underwood, Director, Museum of the Cherokee Indian, Cherokee, North Carolina.

Robert S. Waggoner, St. Louis, Missouri.

Clarence H. Webb, Shreveport, Louisiana.

Bella Weitzner, The American Museum of Natural History, New York, N.Y.

Waldo Wedel, Curator, Division of Archaeology, Smithsonian Institution.

Lester L. Wilson, Wylie, Texas.

Allan Woolworth, Minnesota Historical Society.

F.B. Zahn, Fort Yates, North Dakota; Indian leader and Indian style archer.

Ruth Zahn, Librarian, Missouri Valley College, Marshall, Missouri.

The chapter on the Eskimo Bow and the Asiatic Composite originally appeared in Volume VI, No. 2, 1970, of *Arctic Anthropology,* and is reprinted here with only minor changes by permission of the copyright holders, the Regents of the University of Wisconsin.

And, finally, I must thank my wife, Leone Bailey Hamilton, for seeing this through to completion. She not only typed and retyped the manuscript, and read proof, but has also taken notes throughout the study and proven herself to be a most efficient assistant.

Foreword

The revival of archery as a sport, with its emphasis upon actual hunting or simulated hunting conditions, has revealed to us an entirely new understanding of the bow as a weapon. As an archer I propose to present a new approach to this subject which is often misunderstood in both perspective and terminology by the various disciplines of archaeology, anthropology and ethnology. Those interested in the sport of field archery will, I hope, gain a better background and appreciation of the native archery in the Americas, with particular emphasis upon that area which is now the United States.

Unconsciously, our ideas of marksmanship with either rifle or bow are based upon the Old English shooting standards, which, in turn, evolved from the use of the longbow. No documentary evidence has survived, but the most informed opinion is that the English longbow was perfected during the 13th Century, some hundred years after the Conquest, as a weapon for poaching the Norman deer. It was shot from a standing position and, since it was approximately as long as the shooter's height, it not only permitted, but required, a long draw to get efficient cast. The long cast, which resulted, was not only ideal for shooting deer but proved the longbow to be a perfect weapon when properly used in medieval combat. The English were repeatedly allowed to choose their ground and form their lines, after which the French then made direct frontal attacks against overwhelming firepower. The French never did learn from experience for it is the same story at Crecy, at Poitiers and, with still another variation on the theme, at Agincourt.

There can be no denying that the Old English archer was invincible when defending a fixed position and unsurpassed when poaching the King's deer. But is hitting a standing target at 100 yards, with you own feet firmly planted on the ground, the only standard of excellence in marksmanship? Does it follow that these Old English archers could ride with the Sioux at full gallop and hit a quarter at six feet? Who presumes to say which was the better shot?

The archery of today is actually this Old English shooting tradition crossed with 20th Century engineering and manufacturing techniques. There can be no argument that the resulting hybrid is more efficient in cast — but is it better archery? It seems to me that, when attempting to judge the archery of any time or place, we must consider both the technological stage of development of the people and the materials available to them for bow construction. Then and then only can it be said whether they were good archers or not. It is unreal and pointless to attempt to compare the performance of a longbow or a Plains Indian horse-bow with a modern bow designed from sophisticated experiments by 20th Century engineers in a factory utilizing atomic age materials. Of course the modern bow has the better cast. It would be inexcusable if it did not. Therefore, in evaluating the bowmanship of any people or group care must be taken not to lift it out of its context.

This discussion of aboriginal American bows will not be based upon ethnological areas, but upon somewhat arbitrary geographical divisions. The decision to use geographical areas was based upon the fact that climate, under primitive conditions of trade, is the all-important factor in determining bow design. Kinship, whether by blood or similarities of culture, has practically no influence on bow design if the environment is fundamentally different. An excellent illustration of this will be found in comparing the bows of two branches of the Athapascan-speaking peoples: the Hupa of California and the Apache of Arizona. Both groups used a sinew-lined, reflexed, wooden bow, but the designs of the two bows are so different, because of the methods of hunting and the woods used, that they cannot even be confused in the ethnological literature.

In saying that ethnic relationships will be ignored it is not meant to imply that this is a bloodless investigation of a restricted group of implements. I am not an anthropologist, but an archer, and my interest is how the Indians built their bows and how well they shot. This study is strictly functional, for which I make no apologies.

1

Bow Types and Classification

Bow Action and Terminology. A bow is essentially a two-armed spring spanned by a string. When an arrow is placed on the string and drawn back, energy is stored in the bow. Upon releasing the string, this energy is transmitted directly to the arrow and the arrow is projected into flight. If the same arrow is shot in two bows, any difference between flights of the same arrow must be due to the two bows used, or the way they are handled by the archer. If the archer is skilled, it can be safely assumed that any difference in handling the two bows is negligible, and the primary reason for any difference in flight lies within the bows themselves. This difference in the ability of the bows to project the arrow is spoken of by archers as a difference in "cast."

Cast in a bow is the result of a number of factors. One is the number of pounds of force which must be exerted upon the string to draw the bow back a given distance. For instance, if the string is drawn back until it measures exactly 28 inches from the back of the bow, it is spoken of as a "28 inch draw." If the archer habitually draws the string only 24 inches from the back of the bow, he is said to have a draw of 24 inches. If a good spring scale is substituted for the archer's fingers and the string is drawn back 28 inches and the scale registers 50 pounds, the bow is said to have a "weight" of 50 pounds at 28 inches of draw. The "weight" has nothing to do with the heft of the bow; it merely signifies how many pounds of pull the archer must exert to draw the string back a given number of inches. To have any significance, both weight *and* inches of draw must be stated when speaking of the power of a bow.

However, if two bows of identical weight and draw are used to shoot the same arrow, it is unlikely that the casts will be identical. One bow will throw the same arrow a greater distance every time, in spite of the fact that the two bows are as nearly alike as it is possible to make them; even when they are made of wood from the same tree.

The cast of a bow results not only from a combination of its weight and draw, but also involves the speed with which the bow itself reacts upon the arrow when the string is released. Just why two seemingly identical bows have different casts is difficult to say. In general, we know that certain woods make the best bows. We also know that certain designs are best with given bow-woods, and that various methods of curing the bow-wood result in better or worse cast in the finished bow.

The nomenclature of archery is ancient. Thus the tendency of anthropologists, when writing about bows or archery tackle, to substitute their jargon for standard archers' terminology is inexcusable. To refer, for instance, to the fore end of an arrow or dart shaft as the "distal end" and the nock end as the "proximal end" is, to put it mildly, presumptuous.

When writing or speaking about archery tackle, archery terms should be strictly adhered to. For instance, the "back" of the bow mentioned when discussing the length of draw would normally be referred to as the "front" by the uninitiated, since the back of the bow is the side away from the archer when he shoots. The "belly" is the side facing the archer as he draws. The "limbs" are, obviously, the two arms. There is nothing complicated about archery terms; in this book, each will be explained as the discussion progresses.

As the bow is drawn, the belly of the bow is under compression and the back is under tension. The greater the length of draw, the greater this compression and tension. Back in the days when the archer normally made his own bows, there was a saying that a bow fully drawn was nine-tenths broken. That expresses the condition of the drawn wooden bow perfectly, for a good bow is designed for a given draw. Exceed that draw and the bow will break. This is in reference to the wooden or "self" bow.

The Self-Bow. The self, or simple, bow is made from one piece of wood and depends entirely upon the elasticity of the wooden arms for the cast of the arrow. This is the bow with which everyone is familiar. Most men have made more or less successful self-bows during their boyhood and, when good bow-wood is available and the maker knows how to work down the rough stave, efficient weapons can be produced. The English longbow is the outstanding historical example of this type of bow.

Theoretically, the most efficient cross section for the limb of a wooden bow is an elongated trapezium with the long dimension running from side to side of the bow-limb. This provides great flexibility in the bow-limb, as well as an ample amount of wood fiber to withstand both tension and compression. Since the same cross-sectional area of wood can withstand more tension than compression, the bow-limb should be wider on the belly side than on the back. But

2

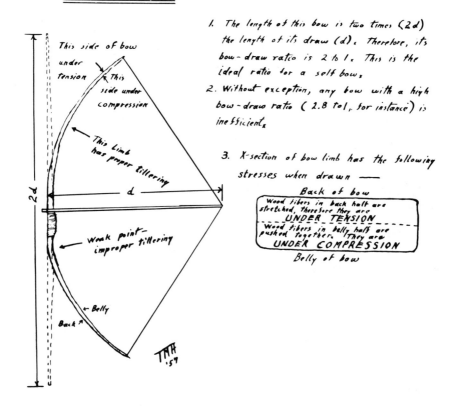

How the self bow works

This side of bow under tension

This side under compression

This limb has proper tillering

This limb has proper tillering

2d

d

Weak point — improper tillering

← Belly

Back →

TNH '57

1. The length of this bow is two times (2d) the length of its draw (d). Therefore, its bow-draw ratio is 2 to 1. This is the ideal ratio for a self bow.

2. Without exception, any bow with a high bow-draw ratio (2.8 to 1, for instance) is inefficient.

3. X-section of bow limb has the following stresses when drawn ——

Back of bow

Wood fibers in back half are stretched, therefore they are
UNDER TENSION
Wood fibers in belly half are pushed together. They are
UNDER COMPRESSION

Belly of bow

FIGURE 1. Some basic factors in self-bow construction.

that is getting down to a rather fine point in design, more important in theory than in practice where a rectangular cross section is a satisfactory compromise.

The English longbow did not conform at all to this ideal, for it had a U-shaped cross section with the rounded part of the U forming the belly of the bow. In other words, where the crushing forces were greatest when the bow was drawn, there was the smallest cross-sectional area to withstand that force. The result was that the wood cells in the belly collapsed to a certain extent after the bow had seen some use, which tended to give the bow a curved shape when it was unstrung. This tendency of the unstrung bow to keep the curved shape of the bow is spoken of as "following the string." Not only the longbow, but all self-bows follow the string to a greater or lesser extent. In general, the better bow-woods follow the string less than the poorer bow-woods. The best bow-wood of all, Osage orange *(Maclura pomifera Sch.)*, follows the string so slightly that it is often hard to detect, while English yew has almost as marked a tendency to follow the string as hickory.

Self-bows with rectangular cross sections in the limbs are known as "flat bows" and the design, which is basically American Indian, practically supplanted the longbow in American archery circles during the 1930's and 40's. This was due to the fact that, since it permitted greater flexing in the bow-limbs, it was possible to build a shorter bow with a sharper cast which gave the arrow a flatter trajectory. Another reason for its popularity was that it was much easier to make than a longbow: a feature which appealed to those of us who made our own shooting gear. We thought then, and I still think, that the greatest pleasure in archery is to spend your winter evenings making your own tackle and when the sun shines to go out and shoot it. To us, a score shot or game killed using modern commercial glass arrows, all absolutely identical in weight and spine, would be meaningless.

Without exception, the best native self-bows I have shot have been flat bows. Aside from a rectangular or flat oval cross section, the only other possible variations would be square, round or the U-shaped cross section with the flat of the U either to the back or belly. The round or the U-shaped cross section *with the flat on the belly side* are the two worst possible designs, and they are often found in native self-bows. In those two types the tensile stresses in the draw are concentrated in a thin line down the center of the rounded back, whereas if the back were flat, these same stresses would be distributed evenly from one side

4

to the other. A good self-bow should *always* have a flat back; the shape of the belly is of secondary importance.

"Tillering" is the shaping of the bow-limb so that every inch, from grip to tip, does its proportionate share of the bending when the bow is drawn and contributes its proportionate share to the cast upon release. After the bow has been roughed out to the point where it can be bent enough to put a string on it, the process of tillering begins. The newly strung bow is drawn enough to show at what points the limb bends too much or too little. Where it is too stiff, the belly is carefully scraped away until the proper curve throughout the length of the limb is achieved.

In proper tillering lies the art of making a good bow. Anyone can make a bow that will shoot after a fashion. It is only the expert bowyer who, after long experience and practice — and with a certain degree of native ability — can tiller a bow so it will deliver the full cast of which it is capable.

Within reasonable limits and other things being equal, the shorter the bow-limbs the greater the cast, because there is less distance for the tips to travel while imparting energy to the arrow. Also, the shorter limb has greater leverage on the string. The energy stored in the bow is released more quickly. That statement applies to bows of all types, not merely to self-bows.

If our primary consideration with a self-bow is the greatest cast and penetration possible, the optimum length of the bow from nock to nock should be twice the length of draw. That means that if a man has a draw of 28 inches and a bow of excellent bow-wood, such as Osage orange, which has been expertly tillered, his best length would be close to 56 inches. It also means, however, that the bow would be working at its extreme limits of stress and in danger of breaking each time it was drawn. Consequently, the practical bow-draw ratio for ordinary working self-bows of good quality should be higher. The two best Osage orange bows of my making have ratios of 2.21 to 1, while my best bow of Indian manufacture has a ratio of 2.26 to 1. It also is of Osage orange, but its draw is only 26 inches while the others are designed for 28.

It is well to fix the bow-draw ratio firmly in mind, for it is a useful point of reference in the study of primitive bows. When working with old self-bows of native manufacture it can be assumed immediately that they did not have a 2 to 1 ratio; that it was probably somewhere around 2.3. Since none of these bows can now be actually drawn, and the draw must be estimated or arrived at by some indirect means, this knowledge enables one to determine immediately the probable length of draw, which he can then refine by other means depending on the evidence available.

Of course, the bow-draw ratio must be used with judgment and common sense. I do not mean to imply that a lower ratio always means a better bow; but, everything considered, it will be found that on the whole the bows with the lower ratios are the more efficient weapons. When examining other more sophisticated types which will be described later, such as the reinforced or the sinew-back bows, it will be found that, in the never-ending struggle for a better cast, many of them did approach the 2 to 1 ratio.

In North America there were two basic forms of the self-bow — the D-bow and the double-curved bow — while in South America there was only the D-bow. The D-bow is simply the plain ordinary bow which everyone thinks of when the word "bow" is mentioned; the curved part of the D represents the bow and the straight part the string. I believe this name was coined by anthropologists and it is quite appropriate.

The term "double-curved" was also first applied by anthropologists. I would have said it was "triple-curved," but their term has become well established and is as good as any other. The outlines of the D-bow and the double-curved are shown in Figure 2, marked D and DC. The latter has the same outline as Cupid's bow, whether it is braced or relaxed. Bracing it merely accentuates the form.

This double-curved outline is achieved by deforming the bow limbs with heat and holding them until cool. Just why this was done — and it appears to have been practiced from coast to coast — is one of the unsolved mysteries of North American archery. Bows of more sophisticated design also had the Cupid's bow outline when braced because there were definite advantages in performance to be gained, but the double-curved self-bow is not as efficient in cast as the ordinary self D-bow. Also, bows with the Cupid's bow outline, regardless of type and almost without exception, buck badly in the hand and are unpleasant to shoot.

There is still a third form of self-bow: the slack-string. To keep the bowstring from injuring the bow hand, a piece of wood was lashed upright at the grip to catch the string. I have been unable to learn anything of interest or importance about this bow from the few casual references so far encountered. It had to be highly inefficient.

The Reinforced Bow. The next step in the evolution of the bow was the introduction of the reinforced bow, which is essentially a self-bow

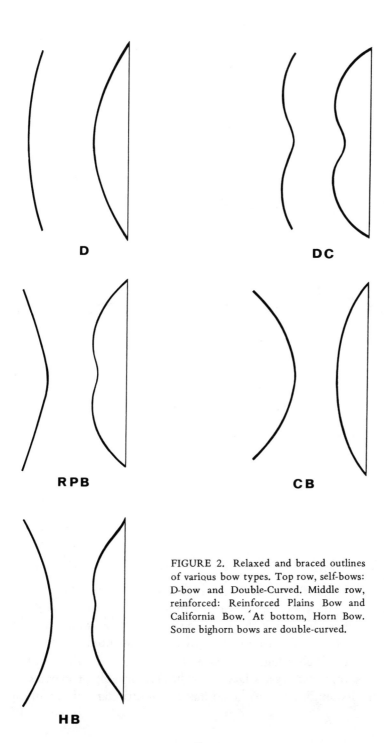

D

DC

RPB

CB

HB

FIGURE 2. Relaxed and braced outlines of various bow types. Top row, self-bows: D-bow and Double-Curved. Middle row, reinforced: Reinforced Plains Bow and California Bow. At bottom, Horn Bow. Some bighorn bows are double-curved.

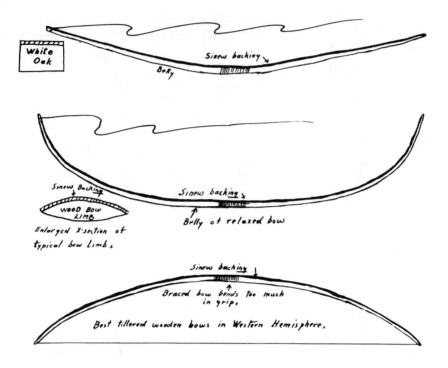

FIGURE 3.   The reinforced Plains bow (top) and the California bow (unstrung and strung), showing the reflex and the sinew backing, or lining. Note characteristic cross sections of the two bows. The bows are not drawn to scale.

with two refinements: the sinew-lining on its back, and the reflex.   The lining, or backing, on these bows consists of a thin layer of sinew glued to the back.   When the bow is drawn, this sinew stretches and not only increases the weight and cast of the bow, but also holds down any splinters of wood which might have a tendency to feather up from the back while it is under tension.   Dry sinew has remarkable properties of elasticity, and its application to bows had a revolutionary effect upon design.

8

The term "reflex" means that the bow-limbs curve or sweep backward from the grip when the bow is relaxed (Figs. 2 and 3). The reflex is, to a certain extent, the result of applying the sinew lining to the back of the wooden bow; as the wet sinew dries it contracts, and in contracting draws the bow limbs back into the reflex. However, in bracing the bow, the limbs must again be brought forward past the face of the belly until the string stands at bracing height, which places high initial tension on the limbs, increasing the efficiency of the cast (Fig. 2 RPB). This will be discussed in more detail in Chapter 4; the point to be made here is that the inefficient double-curved self-bow and the efficient reinforced bow both have the Cupid's bow outline when the latter is braced, even though they are entirely unrelated. When the reinforced bow is relaxed, its limbs immediately assume the reflex, while the double-curved, when relaxed, still shows its deformation.

There were other kinds of reinforced bows made by primitive peoples of the world, such as the laminated bow of the Lapps, but none of these saw service in the Americas. Various forms utilizing sinew on the back, similar in cross section to the American form just described, were used in Asia, but none of them has been described by an archer. Adler's (1902) study of the bows of North Asia is the standard reference, but it leaves many important questions unanswered.

The Composite Bow. The ultimate in bow design was the Asiatic composite, utilizing natural materials by men innocent of an atomic age engineering background. It was the end result of long ages of experimentation in attempting to produce a weapon with a better cast than was possible with the reinforced bow. The interesting thing is that the basic principles of the composite were apparently worked out independently in North America more or less simultaneously with the advent of the horse on the Western Plains around 1700.

The Asiatic composite will be described in detail in Chapter 5, but the composite principle is based upon substituting a relatively non-compressible material (horn) for the belly half of the bow-limb and a remarkably elastic material (sinew) for the back half. Though a foundation strip of wood is used in the center of the limb in the Asiatic composite, the American version dispenses entirely with wood; the sinew-back is glued directly to the horn belly.

Mountain sheep horn and elk antler were the two materials used in the belly of the American composite and the horn invariably represents approximately one-half the thickness of the bow when measured from the surface of the back to that of the belly. The remaining half is the

FIGURE 4. Two views of a bighorn bow from the Nez Perce of Idaho — possibly the best example of this type of bow extant. It is 37-3/4 inches long over all; 1 by 1-1/2 inches wide at the grip, 19/32 by 1-1/2 at mid-limb, and 9/16 by 21/32 immediately below the nock. Like many bighorn bows it is double-curved. *American Museum of Natural History, Catalogue No. 1/2707.*

sinew-back lying in its matrix of glue. This thick sinew-back distinguishes the American composite from the reinforced bow with its thin lining of sinew on its back.

In addition to the American composite there was still another closely related type: the Eskimo bow which, as will be explained in Chapter 5, is definitely a modification of the Asiatic composite to the Arctic environment. This bow, in its better forms, has a foundation of driftwood which also acts as the belly of the bow. The cast was provided by an elaborate system of sinew cords and cables running along the back from nock to nock, with additional cords fastened to the limbs with half hitches and incorporated into the cables as they approached the grip (Figs. 26 and 27).

Bow Classification. The native American bows then can be classified as follows:

A. The self-bow, which depends entirely upon the elasticity of wood for its cast. It is found in three basic forms: (1) the D-bow, (2) the double-curved bow, and (3) the slack-string bow.

B. The reinforced bow, which is essentially a self-bow with a lining of sinew glued to its back. It is found only in the reflexed form.

C. The composite bow, in which horn or antler has been substituted for the wood in the belly half of the limbs and sinew for the back half. A closely related form, also depending entirely upon sinew for cast, is the Eskimo bow. Like the reinforced bows, all composites are reflexed.

Possibly that last statement should be modified by saying that all well designed composites are reflexed. For some unknown reason, certain bighorn bows appear to be double-curved, but are here classified among the American composites until more is known about them (Fig. 4).

2

The Dart and the Arrow

No discussion of native arrows would be complete without first mentioning the dart, and the atlatl with which it was cast, for the arrow is a mere modification of the earlier projectile. Garcilaso, the Spanish-Inca, is the only early writer who reported the use of the atlatl and dart by North American Indians in what now comprises the United States, but since his comments are rather correct in detail, there is no reason to doubt that the weapons' employment in an encounter actually did take place. The fight occurred near the Delta of the Mississippi as the survivors of the De Soto expedition were making their final retreat toward Mexico. (Garcilaso, 1951:597)

"One soldier was wounded with a weapon which the Castilians in the Indies call an arrow, but which I shall call more appropriately a dart since it is thrown with a wooden strip or a cord. Our Spaniards had never seen this weapon before that day in any part of Florida through which they had traveled . . . It is six feet in length, and is fashioned from a reed . . . And in order that the reed of the arrow or dart not be split when a blow is given, they put a knot of thread where it received the tip or harpoon and another on the opposite end at the place which the archers call the 'battle' in the arrow, that place where the shaft received the cord of the bow or the strip with which it is hurled. The strip is of wood two-thirds of a yard in length, and is capable of sending a dart with such great force that it has been seen to pass completely through a man armed with a coat of mail. In Peru, the Spaniards feared this weapon more than any others the Indian possessed for the arrows there were not so fierce as those of Florida."

The "strip of wood two-thirds of a yard in length" is of course the atlatl. It consisted of a grip at one end and a spur, usually of deer horn, set at an angle of about 40 degrees at the other. The dart, which was from about four to five feet in length, had a cup-shaped depression in the butt of the shaft in place of the usual nock found on an arrow. The shaft was placed on the atlatl with the spur fitting into the cup in the butt of the dart shaft; the shaft, in turn, being held in place on the atlatl by two fingers of the throwing hand which grasped the atlatl grip.

The atlatl was cast with an overhand swing, very much as a baseball is thrown; the fingers releasing the dart shaft and allowing the spur in the end of the atlatl to transfer the thrust of the arm to the dart. Since the length of the arm was increased, in effect, by the length of the atlatl, a much higher velocity was in that way imparted to the dart. The principle was exactly the same as when a boy throws green apples or pellets with a switch (Fig. 5).

The atlatl and dart are very, very old, having been in use in Asia and Europe for tens of thousands of years. American archaeologists seem to have established beyond question that the first people to enter the Western Hemisphere carried them as their main weapon, and that they were still in use in what is now the United States until shortly before the arrival of Europeans. They were the favorite weapon of the Aztecs at the time of the Conquest. The bow in America is a recent invention, or introduction — within the last 2,000 years at the very earliest.

For any ancient object of wood, such as an arrow or dart, to be preserved up to our time is a matter of pure luck. When such items are found it is usually due to the fortunate circumstance that the aborigines lost or buried them in dry shelters or caves where no moisture could reach and rot them. Again, sometimes a hunter took a shot at some animal struggling in a tar pit, and those darts have been recovered more or less intact. However they might have been preserved, the fact remains that the total number of atlatls and darts, lost by early man or the later Indians and found by us, is tantalizingly small.

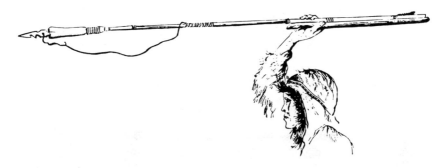

FIGURE 5. How the atlatl, or throwing-stick, was used. *"Throwing-Sticks In The National Museum,"* by Otis T. Mason, *SMITHSONIAN ANNUAL REPORT FOR 1884.*

Strangely enough, many more complete atlatls have been recovered than complete darts. Consequently, the normal length limits for the ancient darts can be set only by inference. As far as the structural details of the darts are concerned, enough fragments have been recovered to enable us to describe them accurately. It must be understood, however, that structural variations occur between individual darts.

The typical dart appears to have been between 50 and 60 inches in length, and one-half inch or more in diameter. It consisted of a dart shaft, which represented the major portion of its over-all length, and a relatively short foreshaft. This foreshaft was always of wood, while the dart shaft proper could be of cane, heavy reed or solid wood. The wooden foreshaft might either be sharpened and serve as the point, or be armed with a point of stone, bone or some other material.

There are two important structural details which must be noted specifically. The first is that the foreshaft was *not* an integral part of the dart. It was inserted into a socket in the front end of the dart shaft and held there with a friction fit (Fig. 6).

Details of Dart Construction

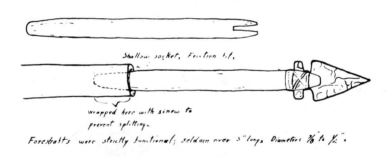

Shallow socket. Friction fit.

wrapped here with sinew to prevent splitting.

Foreshafts were strictly functional; seldom over 5" long. Diameters ⅜" to ½".

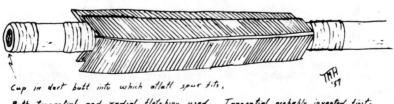

Cup in dart butt into which atlatl spur fits.

Both tangential and radial fletching used. Tangential probably invented first. Dart shafts average 52" to 55" long. Approx. ⅞" dia. at butt and ½" dia. at socket. (After Guernsey & Kidder, 1921 and Harrington, 1933)

FIGURE 6. Construction of dart.

14

The dart shaft represented quite an investment in both time and effort. Furthermore, if the same shaft was cast repeatedly, eventually the thrower could develop a higher degree of accuracy than if he threw a different shaft each time. If the dart shaft was constructed so it fell away easily from the foreshaft, it could be recovered and used again and again. Then only the foreshafts need be changed or replaced as they became lost in wounded animals or broken. Less effort would be required to make replacements and greater accuracy gained in cast.

From the very earliest times (Harrington, 1933:102-4) in the Western Hemisphere wherever the chipped stone point was used, it was mounted on an easily detachable foreshaft. Kidder and Guernsey (1919:182) and Guernsey and Kidder (1921:85-7) discuss this in detail. Harrington (p. 101) found only one armed dart at Gypsum Cave which did not have a foreshaft, but from his comments it appears that he did find in southwestern Texas some simple one-piece darts with stone points.

All the evidence, then, indicates that the foreshaft, when used with the atlatl dart, was strictly functional. When a paleo-Indian went to hunt he probably carried, at most, two dart shafts: one to replace the other if it was broken or carried off by some animal because it failed to drop off the foreshaft. In contrast, he carried a fistful of armed foreshafts to replace those lost or broken in the hunt. Because the dart shaft was relatively large, it was easily recovered, but the foreshafts were constantly in need of replacement.

As with the arrow, in making short casts, fletching is not an absolute necessity on the dart. Malcolm W. Hill (1948:41) is of the opinion that feathering on darts is of no particular benefit on casts up to 50 feet. This coincides with the practice of modern field archers and South American Indians where, in shooting fish at close range, the fletching of the arrow is usually dispensed with. The evidence indicates that the paleo-Indian, when he discovered that he could increase the cast of his throwing spear materially by using the atlatl, quickly hit upon the idea of putting feathers at the rear end to act as a rudder. That is the only purpose of fletching; to act as a rudder or drag to keep the back end from catching up with the front — to keep the projectile from turning or twisting in the air.

Though the basic idea of using feathers to keep the dart or arrow in straight flight has never been improved upon since the day of its inception thousands of years before the introduction of the bow, the method of applying those feathers to the shaft underwent definite improvements. In fact, the latest improvement — the discovery that only a very small surface area of fletching is required to keep an arrow on its course — was not made until the closing years of the 19th century. The excessive feather lengths often observed on arrows of Plains Indian manufacture, for instance, contribute nothing whatever to accuracy and actively work against flight efficiency.

The first attempts at fletching consisted merely of placing a complete tail or wing feather on each side of the shaft and lashing it down flat, fore and aft. Ethnologists have coined the term "tangential fletching" for this form of feather application. The more conventional fletching, where the vanes of the feather are stripped from the quill and then fastened separately to the shaft in a more or less perpendicular position, is spoken of as "radial" fletching.

Tangential fletching is not so efficient as radial. It is more bulky and offers too much wind resistance. It reduces the cast materially because, to use a strictly modern term, there is too much parasitic drag. In contrast, radial fletching can be highly efficient. This does not mean that radial fletching is always highly efficient, as in the case of the excessive feathering on Plains arrows mentioned above; but, taken as a whole, it slows the projectile down much less than the more primitive form.

Heizer (1938:70-1) describes a complete dart found in Pershing County, Nevada, in a layer of bat guano in a rock shelter. The over-all length of this dart is 129.5 cm., or approximately 51 inches. It consists of three pieces: a butt, 38 cm. long and 12 mm. in diameter; a central section 45 cm. long and 9 mm. in diameter; and a foreshaft of greasewood, which also forms the point, 57 cm. long and some 7 mm. in diameter.

That two sections of cane were utilized to make up the shaft was probably due to the absence of a piece of cane of suitable length when the dart was being assembled. Any functional reason for making a dart shaft in two sections is hard to imagine.

The design of the greasewood foreshaft is not so easily explained. It is 57 cm. long, 10.5 of which is inserted into the front end of the center section with a "long, fine cylindrical taper." Obviously, the maker had no intention that this foreshaft should come loose and drop the dart shaft.

The fletching on this particular dart is tangential. Two whole feathers were used, 23.5 cm., or about 9½ inches, long.

Because feathers are highly perishable and are the favorite food of moths and hungry mice, the fletching on ancient darts and arrows is usually difficult to determine. Guernsey and Kidder (1921:84) report that the quills found on dart shafts in White Dog Cave had had the tips cut off and a wooden plug, 1 to 1½ inches long, inserted. The reason for this apparently was to keep from crushing the quill when it was lashed down to the dart shaft and thus help maintain its original angle. They venture no opinion as to whether the fletching was tangential or radial. Heiser (1938:70) believes it to be tangential, and I am just as positive that it is radial. I shall not go into the arguments pro and con concerning this particular dart shaft. The point is that there is room for honest differences of opinion. The great difficulty on this question of tangential versus radial fletching probably stems from a dearth of background information.

It is known positively that in tangential fletching two whole feathers were used in ancient times, and are still being used today in both the Tropics and the Arctic. We are not so sure on the use of three entire feathers. Harrington (1933:95) illustrates the ends of three whole feathers still caught under the lashing on a dart butt from Gypsum Cave (Fig. 7B). There seems to be no question whatever that in this instance there was tangential fletching with three whole feathers. It is quite possible that many other old darts described as having radial fletching, because of the three quills still held under the sinew seizings, actually were tangential.

On most old arrows where the use of a foreshaft is justified, it is utilized for structural convenience rather than for any functional purposes, as with the dart. When the arrow is made of reed, as in our Southwest, or of cane, as in the rain forests of South America, it is obvious that a foreshaft of wood must be utilized to act as a point itself, or carry a point of some other material. It is simply not practical to mount an arrowhead directly on the hollow reed or cane arrow shaft.

However, when an otherwise functional foreshaft in a reed or cane arrow assumes an exaggerated length, it is evidence of traditional rather than practical traits. So long as a particular foreshaft serves a practical purpose only upon a particular arrow shaft, it is functional. When it cannot be justified upon functional grounds, the foreshaft should be considered traditional. Unlike the footed arrow, which is of uniform diameter throughout, the foreshafted arrow in the bow is drawn only to the splice. The foreshaft overhangs the bow hand. The non-functional, or traditional, foreshaft adds in no way to the depth of penetration by the arrow, and it serves no useful purpose.

Practically all foreshafted arrows in the temperate zone of North America were non-functional, except for the reed arrows of the Apache and Pueblo areas as well as certain arrow types found in the Pacific

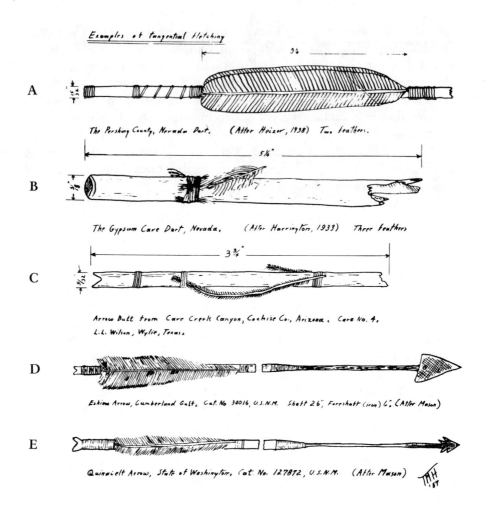

Examples of tangential fletching

A

The Pershing County, Nevada Dart. (After Heizer, 1938) Two feathers.

B

The Gypsum Cave Dart, Nevada. (After Harrington, 1933) Three feathers

C

Arrow Butt from Cave Creek Canyon, Cochise Co., Arizona, Cave No. 4, L.L. Wilson, Wylie, Texas.

D

Eskimo Arrow, Cumberland Gulf, Cat. No 38016, U.S.N.M. Shaft 26", Foreshaft (iron) 6", (After Mason)

E

Quinaielt Arrow, State of Washington, Cat. No. 127872, U.S.N.M. (After Mason)

FIGURE 7. Tangential fletching.

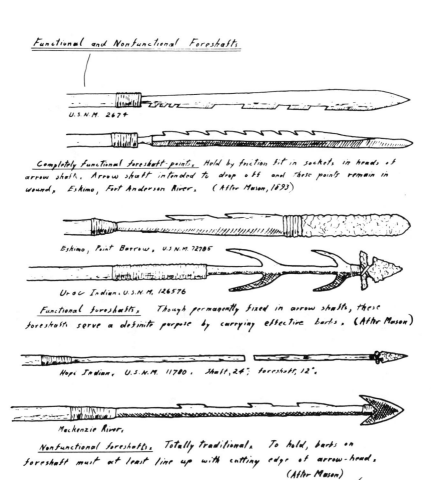

Functional and Nonfunctional Foreshafts

U.S.N.M. 2674

Completely functional foreshaft-points. Held by friction fit in sockets in heads of arrow shaft. Arrow shaft intended to drop off and these points remain in wound. Eskimo, Fort Anderson River. (After Mason, 1893)

Eskimo, Point Barrow, U.S.N.M. 72785

Uroc Indian, U.S.N.M. 126576

Functional foreshafts. Though permanently fixed in arrow shafts, these foreshafts serve a definite purpose by carrying effective barbs. (After Mason)

Hopi Indian, U.S.N.M. 11700. Shaft, 24"; foreshaft, 12".

Mackenzie River.

Nonfunctional foreshafts. Totally traditional. To hold, barbs on foreshaft must at least line up with cutting edge of arrow-head.
(After Mason)

TNH '57

FIGURE 8. Foreshafts.

19

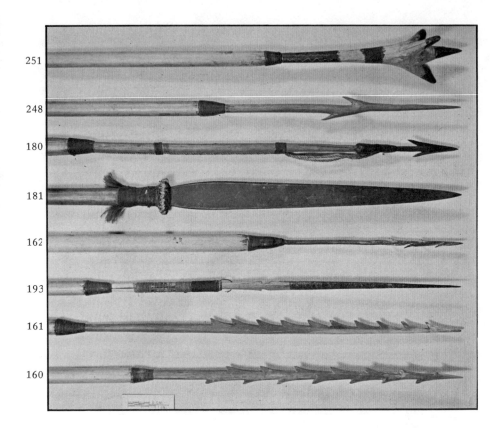

FIGURE 9A. Head ends of Wai Wai arrows, Guyana:

(251) A blunt used to stun large birds.

(248, 161 and 160) Arrows with barbed foreshaft points used in shooting small game such as agouti and monkey. These are from 175 to 198.5 cm. long and weigh approximately 2-1/4 ounces.

(180) The harpoon arrow being shot by the Indian in Fig. 20. It is 181 cm. (71 in.) long, weighs 2-1/4 ounces.

(181) A spear arrow used in shooting tapir only. 198 cm. (78 in.) long.

(162) The fish arrow being used in Fig. 19.

(193) A poisoned arrow used especially in shooting monkeys. 206.5 cm. (81 in.) long, 2-1/2 ounces.

20

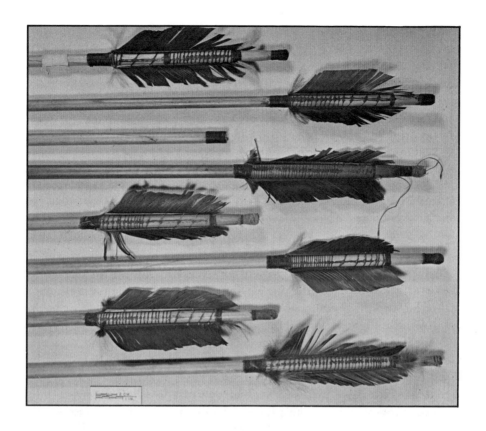

FIGURE 9B.   The nock ends of arrows at left. *Photographs and information courtesy Clifford Evans and Betty Meggers, Smithsonian Institution.*

States.   On the other hand, some Eskimo foreshafts — or perhaps we should say foreshaft-points — were designed to enter the wound and drop the arrow exactly as the ancient foreshaft was intended to drop the dart shaft.   This is not surprising since the Eskimos still used the atlatl and dart in their hunting, and the harpoon was nothing more than a heavy dart without the fletching.

The differences between the functional and non-functional foreshafts are illustrated in Fig. 8.   All drawings are copied from Mason's (1893) monumental NORTH AMERICAN BOWS, ARROWS AND QUIV-ERS.   The arrow in Fig. 7,E is particularly interesting.   In this case the foreshaft is an iron wire whose end has been flattened by hammering and then filed to a point.   It is, nevertheless, a non-functional foreshaft.

In contrast with the arrows which have just been discussed, many of the long, dart-like arrows of South America have functional foreshafts. Various arrowheads used by the Wai Wai of British Guiana definitely come under this classification (Fig. 9).

Today it is our custom in fletching to apply the strip of quill, upon which the vane of the feather directly stands, to the wood of the shaft and hold it there with glue. This appears to have been also the accepted way of fletching among the Old English. Back in 1603 Martin Pring (1906) had the following to say in describing the arrows of the Indians which he saw in what is now New England.

"Their arrowes are of a yard and an handfull long, not made of Reeds, but of a fine light wood very smooth and round with three long and deepe blacke feathers of some Eagle, Vulture, or Kite, as closely fastened with some binding matter, as any Fletcher of ours can glue them on . . . . ."

If the vanes are applied to the arrow shaft with reasonable uniformity of alignment, if they are glued securely to the shaft, and if the vanes themselves do not present an excessive amount of surface to the wind, then we have the more efficient form of tangential fletching. Either loose flappy vanes, or exceedingly long and wide vanes, or both, cut down the flight efficiency of the arrow.

Some Plains arrows have so much feather in the fletching that this alone is good evidence that the maker never made long shots. When feathering is carried to such extremes it does not take a scientist to detect the difference in cast. Such arrows can be used effectively only on short shots where the shaft has reached its mark before the retarding action, induced by the drag of the fletching, can take marked effect.

An entirely different type of inefficient radial fletching is that practiced among some of the South American Indians; specifically, the Wai Wai and others in British Guiana. Roth (1916, Plates 19 and 20) shows exactly how these feather vanes are lashed to the shaft. Four separate and distinct lashings are used in this area and Roth designates them as the diamond, the claw, the bar and the spiral. Apparently, the Wai Wai fletching is lashed down with what Roth would call the spiral attachment (Fig. 9). Incidentally, only two feather vanes are ordinarily used by these Indians (Roth, 1916:159), and Roth says that the spiral lashing is "the quickest but laziest pattern to follow."

The specific construction of the aboriginal, or pre-contact, arrows in various areas of the Western Hemisphere is rather hard to determine with any accuracy at this late date. The natural hazards which work against the preservation of atlatl darts also apply to arrows. As with darts, most of the older arrows which have been recovered came from dry shelters and dry caves in the western part of North America.

A good example is found among arrow fragments salvaged from a series of small caves in Arizona by Lester L. Wilson of Wylie, Texas (Fig. 10). Unfortunately, these caves had been thoroughly ransacked by

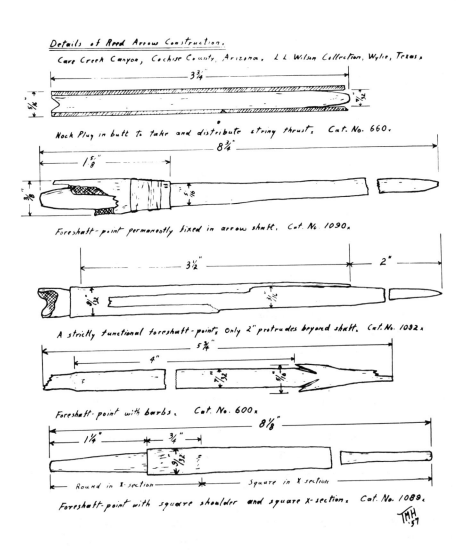

Details of Reed Arrow Construction.

Care Creek Canyon, Cochise County, Arizona. L L Wilson Collection, Wylie, Texas.

Nock Plug in butt To take and distribute string thrust. Cat. No. 660.

Foreshaft-point permanently fixed in arrow shaft. Cat. No. 1090.

A strictly functional foreshaft-point. Only 2" protrudes beyond shaft. Cat. No. 1032.

Foreshaft-point with barbs. Cat. No. 600.

Foreshaft-point with square shoulder and square x-section. Cat. No. 1089.

FIGURE 10. Primitive arrow fragments found in Arizona caves.

relic hunters, and any evidence of stratification destroyed, so Mr. Wilson is unable to estimate the probable age of these pieces. However, because of the primitive characteristics which they show, there is every reason to believe they have a respectable antiquity.

The nock ends of five reed arrows are illustrated (Fig. 11). No. 1 is distinguished primarily by its size. At its greatest diameter it measures 5/16 of an inch. The nock is formed by inserting a solid wooden plug in the open end of the reed and then cutting a shallow "v" notch across the butt. Three feather quills are still held under the sinew lashing.

No. 2 is made exactly like No. 1 except for size. It is only 7/32 of an inch in diameter, but also had three vanes in a radial fletching.

The surrounding reed has broken away from the wooden plug in the nock of No. 4, so that the construction is seen.

No. 5 is a nock with tangential fletching. On this arrow two whole feathers from some small bird were used. These feathers measure only 2 inches in length and the feather barbs are quite narrow. If this was the original width of the individual feathers, and they have not been reduced through the action of moths or mice, this particular fletching could not have been too effective. However, it is unmistakably tangential.

Below the nocks are shown two of the smaller foreshafts picked up in the debris left in these caves. The first foreshaft, again because of the breaking away of the surrounding reed arrow shaft, shows how the wooden point was inserted in the hollow end until it butted up against the natural partition formed in the node of the reed. In this instance the wooden point is 5½ inches long and is inserted 3½ inches into the reed shaft. Therefore, with this arrow the non-functional foreshaft has been avoided and only the wooden point retained.

The last item is a broken foreshaft in which two opposing barbs have been whittled. In this case some attempt was made to utilize the foreshaft. It would be interesting to know whether it was originally armed with a wooden point, like the others from these caves, or had an arrowhead of some other material.

It is indeed unfortunate that there is no way of telling just what the lengths of these arrows were, but their relationship to the arrows still being used in the rain forests of South America is obvious (see Chapter III).

The structural similarities to the ancient atlatl darts are also evident. The larger arrow sections could easily have been darts; the only actual difference is a notch in the butt in place of a cup to fit the spur on the atlatl.

FIGURE 11. Reed arrow fragments from Cave Creek Canyon, Cochise Canyon, Ariz. (see Fig. 10). The upper five are nock ends, while the lower two are wooden points. Note that part of reed has broken away from the fourth, revealing how the wooden plug was inserted to distribute the thrust of the bowstring.

The arming of the arrow is a study in itself. The chipped stone point is ordinarily thought of when we speak of an "arrowhead," but, in practice, many other things were used beside flint or chert. The Gentleman of Elvas, who was on De Soto's expedition, says that "some [arrows] are pointed with the bone of a fish . . . and others with some stone like a point of a diamond." John Smith in his DESCRIPTION OF VIRGINIA only mentions "flints or splinters of stone, in form of a heart, an inch broad and an inch and a half or more long." But in spite of the fact that the early explorers were impressed primarily with the stone arrowheads, a glance at any archaeological collection shows that arrowheads were made also of antler, animal bone and copper. And our museums are full of Indian arrows of historic times which are armed with wooden heads.

These wooden arrowheads are not the same as an unarmed arrow. The term "unarmed arrow" means an arrow without any head whatever. The shaft, or foreshaft, may or may not be pointed, or it may or may not be charred in the fire. On the other hand, the wooden arrowhead may either be carved out of the foreshaft itself or from a separate piece of wood and placed on the shaft.

At least in historic times, these wooden arrowheads were as widespread as the chipped stone points. They are found on Eskimo arrows and on arrows from the rain forests of South America. They were used on the West Coast, and they are found in collections made along the Canadian border around the Great Lakes. The only place where they are not in evidence seems to be among the Plains Indians.

American archaeologists have tended to assume in recent years that there was a definite limit to the size of the chipped stone arrowhead which an Indian bow could handle and that, therefore, the smaller projectile points were used on arrows and the larger on darts. From other bits of evidence some archaeologists have concluded that the bow was introduced into North America relatively recently — possibly as late as 1000 A.D. — and an analysis of projectile points found on Indian village sites, where the occupational debris has not been disturbed, proves that the small projectile points are invariably found in the upper, or later, layers of the deposit.

This assumption has been attacked from time to time by archers. However, upon examining their arguments it is found that these archers are so accustomed to thinking in terms of the Old English archery standards that the equipment they used to demonstrate the assumed errors in reasoning by the archaeologists is basically Old English in type, usually with modifications resulting from 20th Century engineering research. Obviously, if one is trying to demonstrate how big a projectile point an Indian arrow can accommodate he must forget the Old English archery traditions and use tackle like that the Indian actually used.

That the Indian bow and the Indian arrow did handle a heavy projectile point, after a fashion, is demonstrated by examining any museum collection. However, it will be found that every Indian arrow armed with a large, heavy point has the arrow shaft fitting into some sort of socket in the point. On the other hand, where the arrow shaft is split or notched to receive the projectile point, as is necessarily the case with a chipped stone arrowhead, the diameter of the shaft places a definite limit upon the thickness of the arrowhead which can be wedged into the split or notch. Therefore, it is not the weight or the over-all dimensions of the projectile point which determine how large it can be to be shot in a bow, but how it is to be mounted on the arrow shaft. In the case of a chipped stone projectile point, the critical dimension is the thickness of the stem of the point, which, in actual practice on Indian arrows, seldom is over 3/16 of an inch.

3

The Self Bow

Except in the Arctic, the self-bow was used throughout the Americas, and in North America it was the only type used east of the Mississippi. In general this area was covered with a hardwood forest furnishing dependable supplies of bow-woods: hickory, ash and black locust probably being the most popular. Along the Mississippi, south from the present state of Missouri, the best of all bow-woods, Osage orange, would have been available.

Since this area was the first to be settled or, at least, invaded by the white trader, the bow, as a serious weapon, has long since disappeared; our museums today are almost entirely lacking in aboriginal, or near aboriginal, specimens. The haste with which the natives east of the Mississippi abandoned the bow in favor of the gun is in marked contrast to the way the Plains Indians continued to rely upon the bow into the third quarter of the 19th Century. From this we can conclude that either the bow of the Eastern woodlands was not so effective or the conditions of war and hunting were not so favorable to its use.

As a matter of perspective, Jamestown was settled in 1607. La Salle was building his post, known as Fort St. Louis, on the Illinois River in 1681, and other Frenchmen had established Fort Orleans on the Missouri, some eighty miles east of present-day Kansas City, by 1723. Therefore, it can safely be said that by 1700 every Indian from the Atlantic to the Mississippi had heard of the gun and was clamoring for one, and the art of making good bows went into a rapid decline.

The moment the report of the first gun was heard in any given area, the entire hunting complex changed. No longer was it possible for the hunter to move silently among the game, making his kill quietly and without arousing alarm. The scene shown in the frontispiece of Indians stalking deer was observed by Le Moyne, one of the earliest eyewitnesses of the habits and customs of the natives along the Atlantic Coast, and it is an accurate depiction of deer hunting under aboriginal conditions. But loud noises arouse panic and the game quickly associates the noise with the cause, whether the "cause" himself happens to be the proud possessor of a gun or not. The result is that the game, which formerly could be stalked easily, becomes shy and the man, whose family depends upon his skill as a hunter, must have a gun in order to get his share of the meat as well as hides to trade for still more guns.

The only exception to this generalization was the buffalo. Though buffalo are said to have ranged as far east as present New York State, I have been unable to find any contemporary accounts of hunting them east of the Mississippi; but when the herds were being exterminated on the Western Plains during the 1870's the most efficient method of killing was for the hunter to make his approach from the downwind side, conceal himself, lay out his cartridges conveniently before him on the ground, and go to work. So long as the herd did not get the scent of the hunter or his gun, it stood quietly grazing until the last one dropped. But with the horse enabling the hunter to ride up to point-blank, the bow remained the dominant weapon on the Plains until the introduction of the revolver in the 1850's.

Even a casual examination of the Eastern bows now reposing in the storerooms of our museums bears out their rapid decline as a serious weapon. Most of these specimens were uncritically collected toward the close of the 19th Century; the attitude of the collector apparently being that a bow was a bow. Such an eminent anthropologist as John R. Swanton in his INDIAN TRIBES OF THE LOWER MISSISSIPPI VALLEY (1911, Plate 8) illustrates his work with a picture of an Indian informant posed with what is obviously some child's toy weapon. In this same work Swanton shows on page 347 a Chitimacha bow which "may represent some ancient forms." It represents nothing other than that the tribe could no longer make bows; the whip-ended object shown being about as effective as one made from an umbrella rib.

The Sudbury bow, now in the Peabody Museum, Harvard University, is the only museum specimen I have found which appears to be representative of an aboriginal, or near aboriginal, weapon (Fig. 12). The following inscription, written in ink and now badly faded, is on the belly.

"This bow was taken from an Indian in Sudbury, Mass., A.D. 1660 by William Goodnough who shot the Indian while he was ransacking the Goodnough house for plunder. Presented to the A.A. Society by the Rev. Charles H. Crosby in April 29, 1826."

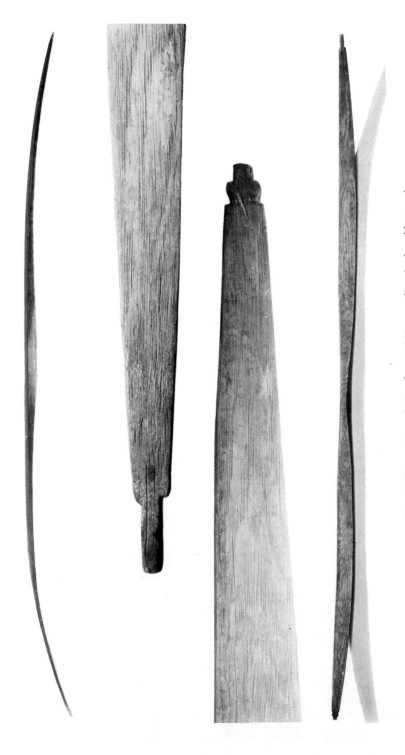

FIGURE 12. The Sudbury Bow, dating from 1660 or earlier, is the oldest native self-bow known to the author. It is a well tillered weapon. *Photo courtesy Peabody Museum, Harvard University. Catalogue No. 49340.*

Dr. Robert E. Greengo, while still at Peabody some years ago, obtained the dimensions of this bow for me. They are as follows:

Length, nock to nock . . . . 65 inches
Length over-all . . . . 67-1/8 inches
Grip . . . .,. 1-3/16″ x 15/16″ wide
Midway from grip to nock
  Upper limb . . . . 9/16″ x 1-7/8″ wide
  Lower limb . . . . 9/16″ x 1-3/4″ wide
Below nocks
  Upper limb . . . . 3/8″ x 3/4″ wide
  Lower limb . . . . 5/16″ x 3/4″ wide

The side and belly views in Fig. 12 are excellent, but the bow must be seen to be appreciated. It is of hickory and beautifully tillered; the pronounced set from following the string is probably due to its having been left braced for many years after it was taken from the dead Indian. Saxton Pope (1923:353) secured an outline drawing and dimensions of this bow from Professor Kroeber in the 1920's and made an exact replica from a dense-grained, well-seasoned stave of red hickory. This replica had a weight of 46 pounds at 28 inches of draw and a cast of 173 yards. Pope's conclusion was that "it is soft and pleasant to shoot, and could do effective work either as a hunting or a war implement."

Since other museum specimens similar to the Sudbury bow have not been found, there are only two other possible sources of information on the native bows of that period: the drawings of artists who were eyewitnesses, and the chronicles of early explorers. The evidence to be found in the drawings must be used with circumspection, for one can never be quite certain when the artist was depicting what he actually saw and when he was merely drawing what he thought he saw.

To the Englishmen of the late 1500's and early 1600's, the longbow was still an everyday weapon with which any man pretending to military experience was well acquainted. It can be argued that the longbow is seldom mentioned in the old chronicles, but neither is the arquebus, or harquebus as it was usually termed. The early English explorers do speak of so many "harquebus shots distant," but just as often they speak in terms of "bow shots." They were writing for their contemporaries and not for posterity, so they saw no reason to single out the longbow because they assumed their readers would know it was present and used in the company's armament.

This makes the two paintings by John White, governor of Virginia (Figs. 13, 14) , all the more interesting, as well as De Bry's engraving made from White's "An Indian Chief" (Fig. 15A). To me the weapons carried by these natives look suspiciously like English longbows. The question is: Did White's subjects actually carry such powerful, well tillered bows, or did he merely sketch them in as a sort of afterthought, relying more upon his own intimate knowledge of the English weapon? I frankly do not know.

Father Andrew White (1907), in his BRIEF RELATION OF A VOYAGE UNTO MARYLAND, 1639, says: "Their bow is but weake and shoots level but a little way." John Smith (1907:104) states that "Forty yards will they shoot levell, or very neare the mark, and 120 is their best at Random." On the other hand, in this same general geographical area, Percy (1907) gives a diametrically opposite evaluation, but with humorous overtones:

"One of our gentlemen having a Target which he trusted in ... he set it up against a tree, willing one of the Savages to shoot; who took from his backe an Arrow of an elle long, drew it strongly in his Bowe, shoots the Target a foote thorow or better: which was strange, being that a Pistoll could not pierce it. We seeing the force of his Bowe, afterwards set him up a steel Target; he shot again, and burst his arrow all to pieces. He presently pulled out another Arrow, and bit it in his teeth, and seemed in a great rage; so he went away in a great anger."

The "Target" referred to was a small shield. James Rosier (1906) also made some interesting comparisons between English and Indian shooting:

"When we went ashore to trade with them, in one of their Canoes I saw their bowes and arrowes, which I took up and drew an arrow in one of them, which I found to be of a strength able to carry an arrow five or sixe score stronglie; and one of them took it and drew as we draw our bowes, not like the Indians. Their bow is made of wich Hazell and some of Beech in a fashion like our bowes, but they want nocks, onely a string of leather put through a hole at one end, and made fast with a knot at the other."

These statements simply cannot be reconciled. Smith's 120 yards, which was his Indian's "best at Random," is the same distance as Rosier's "sixe score stronglie." The former was implying a weak bow, while the latter was describing a bow any Englishman of that day would respect, for its cast would be far beyond "sixe score."

The most concrete information we have today concerning the actual

FIGURE 13. "An Indian Chief," water color by Gov. John White of Virginia. In this and other portraits by White, the bows are questionable. They may have been influenced by his knowledge of English longbows. *THE NEW WORLD, by Stefan Lorant.*

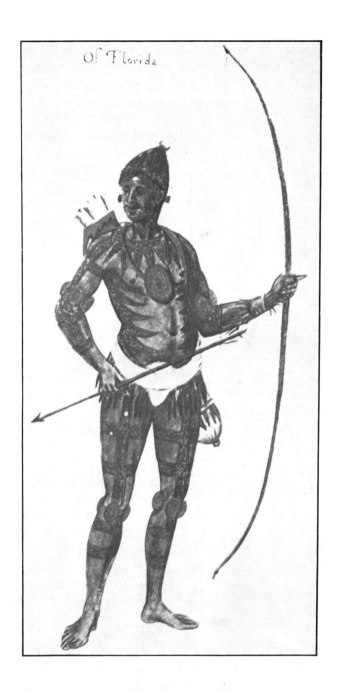

FIGURE 14. "A Warrior of Florida," another water color
by Gov. John White of Virginia. John Hawkins described
the bows of these Indians as "not greatly inferior to
ours." *THE NEW WORLD, by Stefan Lorant.*

distances normally shot by English archers is to be found in "A Plan of All the Marks belonging to the Company of Finsbury Archers," made in 1737 by Daines Barrington (1785: 46-68). Finsbury was an ancient shooting-field still lying, at that time, near the outskirts of London. The shots ranged from 3 score, 13 yards, to 13 score, 5, with most of them clustering between 8 and 10 score. From this it is seen that Rosier's bow could have done creditable work on most of the butts at Finsbury Field, but it could not handle the more powerful shots. Therefore, it is entirely possible that John White was accurately depicting a typical native bow of that immediate area when he painted "An Indian Chief."

Before leaving Rosier it is interesting to note that he says the native bows did not have nocks; that the bowstring passed through a hole on one tip and was tied at the other when the bow was braced. This tying and untying of the bowstring seems to have been an almost universal practice in the Americas, for the usual loop was never used by our Plains Indians. When they braced their bows, they first soaked the end of the sinew string thoroughly in their mouths and then made the tie while it was soft and pliable. Others used a noose, rather than a loop.

While De Bry's "A Weroans, or Chieftain, of Virginia" is a rather faithful copy of White's "An Indian Chief," there are two differences in detail worth noting (Figs. 13, 15A, 15B). First, De Bry has given the bow a fancy nock not in White's original, and second, the bow is too thick in proportion to its length. This seems to be a more or less constant failing of De Bry, for most of the bows shown in his engravings after Le Moyne are also impossibly thick and club-like; his "Saturiba Goes to War" fortunately being an exception.

Le Moyne was a Frenchman and there is no reason to presume he was as familiar with the bow as his English contemporaries. The scene in Fig. 16 is based on one of his paintings, now lost. Two types of typical native self-bows are shown: the D-bow and the double-curved. Since the double-curved bow is strictly a North American type, there can be no question that Le Moyne here faithfully depicted what he saw. Even the loops on the bowstrings may be authentic.

Recently, a self-bow was recovered by Webb and McKinney (1963) from a burial on the Mounds Plantation site, Caddo Parish, La., site No. 16-Cd12. The estimated age of the burial, based upon two carbon 14 dates, is 1050-1070 A.D. and the cultural association is Alto-Gahagan focus, Gibson Aspect (Early Caddoan). In a letter dated 4 April 1967 Dr. Webb states that the bow is made of Osage orange; the over-all

FIGURE 15A. Engraving by De Bry after Governor White's "An Indian Chief" (Fig. 13). *THE NEW WORLD,* *by Stefan Lorant.*

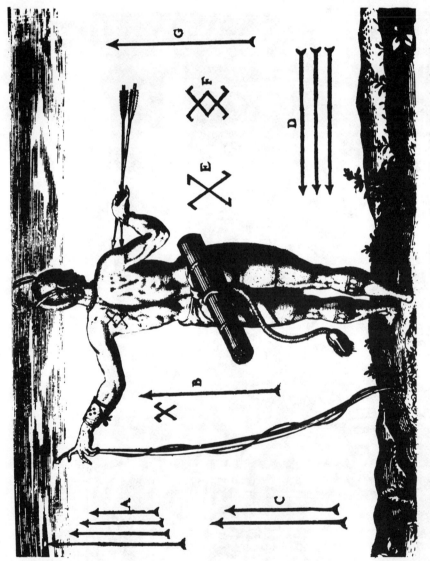

FIGURE 15B. Another engraving by De Bry after Governor White. In this and Fig. 15A, note that bows have nocks not in White's original, and that bows are too thick. *THE NEW WORLD, by Stefan Lorant.*

length is 66 inches with a grip diameter of 1-1/4 inches. One limb is badly decayed, but the better half indicates that its cross section at the center of the limb was circular. The outline of the bow has been distorted by burial, but the better preserved half indicates that it was a simple D-bow with recurved tips. The bow is in the possession of Ralph McKinney. No detailed description of this bow has been published; the reference given merely mentions the bow in association with other materials recovered.

The significance of this D-bow lies in its similarity to the D-bows with recurved tips shown in the De Bry engraving (Fig. 16). A rough pencil sketch in the margin of Dr. Webb's letter matches the De Bry bow perfectly and fortifies my faith in the accuracy of that particular picture.

John White's "A Warrior of Florida" is again armed with what appears to be an English longbow (Fig. 14). As a drawing of a bow it is, if anything, better proportioned than the one shown in "An Indian Chief." There seems to be some question as to whether White actually visited these natives or copied some painting by Le Moyne, but, since all but one of Le Moyne's paintings have been lost, there is no way of deciding this. Anyway, in 1565 John Hawkins (1906) visited this same area and had the following observation to make concerning the native archers near the St. John's River:

"In their warres they use bowes and arrowes, whereof their bows are made of a kind of yew, blacker than ours, and for the most part passing the strength of the Negros and Indians, for *it is not greatly inferior to ours:* Their arrowes are also of a great length, but yet of reeds like other Indians, but varying in two points, both in length and also for nocks and feathers, which the other lacks, whereby they shoot very stedy . . ." (My italics.)

Laudonniere (1907:73-4) describes a fight in 1566 from which the French were able to escape only by the expedient of breaking every arrow which fell near them and in that way gradually depriving the pursuing Indians of the benefit of being able to replenish their supply. The Spanish accounts, covering their early explorations in what is now Southeastern United States, are not much more helpful. Garcilaso, who is the most quoted, got all his information at second hand, but his greatest failing is that he was more interested in telling tall stories than sticking with the facts. The Gentleman of Elvas sensibly observed that unarmed arrows — those without arrowheads — were more to be feared than armed, since the shafts splintered upon hitting the Spanish chain

FIGURE 16. "Saturiba Goes to War," an engraving by De Bry after a lost painting by Le Moyne. The double-curved bow at left indicates that this is an accurate representation of Indian life as seen by early European visitors on the East Coast. This type of self-bow was confined to North America. *THE NEW WORLD, by Stefan Lorant.*

40

mail and the resulting splinters caused severe wounds. Cabeza de Vaca (1907) is almost as unreliable as Garcilaso, for bows "as thick as the arm" and "eleven or twelve palms" (44 to 48 inches) in length don't discharge arrows "at two hundred paces with so great precision that they miss nothing." Anything as stiff as that may make a good club, but not a bow.

There is a bow in my collection which may or may not be significant. All that can be said positively is that it was collected some seventy-five years ago among the Five Civilized Tribes in Oklahoma. Since these Indians were removed to Oklahoma from Southeastern United States, it is just possible that this bow is an ancient heirloom or it may represent the aboriginal type used in that area and made before the art of bowmaking was lost.

It is strictly a no-nonsense weapon made of Osage orange; 60-1/2 inches long over-all, 59-1/2 inches between nocks, rectangular in cross-section, 1-1/2 x 3/4 inches at the grip, 1-1/8 x 3/8 inches at midarm, and 11/16 x 3/8 inches just below the nocks. The belly is slightly rounded and the back flat, with no attempt made to follow the grain. The only concession to elegance is that the edges of the wood have been shaved off slightly so there are no raw corners. It is double-curved and the sinew bowstring has a loop.

Some years ago I made up a linen bowstring for this bow and tried it out. The bow has a weight of about 50 pounds at 26 inches of draw. It was definitely designed for that draw, for the weight increases disproportionately if taken to 28 inches. At 26 inches it cast a 30-gram hunting arrow 159 yards, and, like most double-curved bows, it bucked badly upon release. It is not a pleasant bow to shoot. With a regular flight arrow it probably would reach 200 yards.

West of the Mississippi we have more exact information on the aboriginal bow than to the east. Many bows, both fragmentary and complete, have been recovered by archaeologists working in the Great Basin and the Southwest because of the more arid climatic conditions. Early Spanish references to the self-bow are as ambiguous as in the Southeast; but several excellent comments concerning the bow in its final stage of development were left by American adventurers during the first half of the 19th Century. There are also many of these later self-bows in storage or on display in museums. By comparing these later horse-bows with the earlier archaeologically-recovered foot-bows, a reasonably accurate picture of the development emerges.

Guernsey (1931: 99-107) illustrates one Pueblo I and two Pueblo III bows. The Pueblo I bow is 61-1/8 inches long and has a grip diameter of

1-1/8 inches. "It is made of a section of a sapling unaltered except for removing the bark and tapering the ends." One of the Pueblo III bows can be dismissed, since it obviously was a boy's bow and is little more than a plain stick 46 inches long. The other Pueblo III bow is 54-1/2 inches long and measures 1-3/8 x 1 inch at the grip. "One surface of the belly of the bow is unfinished, save for the bark and twigs. The back is flattened. It is tapered at the ends, which have shallow notches for the reception of the string."

Whether or not the lapse in time between Pueblo I and III had anything to do with it, the Pueblo III bow shows a definite improvement in design. In the Pueblo I bow the tensile stresses, when the bow was drawn, concentrated along the center line of the rounded back; a flat back, as in the Pueblo III bow, spreads these stresses across the entire surface. This is an important design feature in self-bows.

C.B. Cosgrove (1947) describes 41 bows recovered from caves in the upper Gila and Heuco areas, breaking them down into three types. The five Type I bows were round in cross section throughout their entire length, which averaged about 54 inches. The seven Type 2 bows had flat backs and round bellies throughout their length, averaging 45 inches. The twenty-nine Type 3 bows had round center sections representing one-half to one-third of the over-all length, with the remainder of the limbs with flat backs. These bows were from 49 to 56 inches long. Since all these bows used three-strand yucca fiber bowstrings, their performance could not have been very impressive.

The Spiro mound (Hamilton, 1952), with a radiocarbon date of 1200 to 1300 A.D., contained some engravings made on conch shells of men carrying bows. The illustration shows unmistakably that the bows are long and are being held with the lower tip either resting on the ground or close to it (Fig. 17).

David Thompson (1916:328-9) describes a fight between the Piegan and Shoshone in pre-horse days, as told to him by an aged native. From this account, it seems that these bows were approximately 5 feet long, because it is indicated that they would reach to the chin.

From these and other bits of evidence the probabilities are that the aboriginal bows of the West, like those of the East, tended to be long, but not excessively so; the average length being close to 5 feet.

Even after the horse had spread across the Plains there were, of course, many Indians who remained primarily afoot; among the Pueblos and along the Pacific Coast, for instance, bows showed little change until finally supplanted by the gun. But wherever the horse became a

42

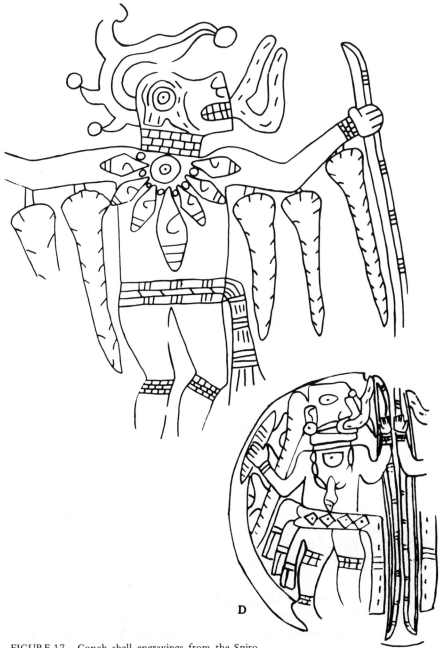

D

FIGURE 17. Conch shell engravings from the Spiro mound, Spiro, Okla., demonstrating the length of precontact bows. Contents of the mound have been dated from 1200 to 1300 A.D. by Carbon 14 tests. *THE SPIRO MOUND, by Henry W. Hamilton.*

fundamental part of the Indian culture, there was immediate pressure to modify the bow to this new method of hunting and fighting.

Where a self-bow is concerned, everything else being equal, a long bow permits a long draw which, in turn, means a long cast. And a long cast is·most desirable to a man who must hunt and fight on foot. But when that same man mounts a horse and can ride up to point-blank range before releasing his arrow into a buffalo, he gains several advantages. One is a more certain kill and another is fewer lost arrows. In short, the standard of living goes up and the cost goes down.

But to hunt or fight on horseback requires a shorter bow. If a self-bow is being used, the bow-draw ratio is around 2.3 to 1 to start with and this means that, as the bow is shortened to accommodate its use on the horse, so is the draw. Obviously, there must be a definite limit beneath which the bow cannot be shortened and still have enough power left in the draw to kill the buffalo.

The successful self horse-bow provides an interesting study showing how delicately the factors of length, draw, weight and cast balance each other. Needless to say, some of the self-bows made by the Plains Indians were dismal failures, but many others were highly successful. The four double-curved self-bows in the collection of the Nebraska State Historical Society are excellent examples of the better self-bows of the Plains Indians (Fig. 18).

Francis La Flesche, in an article reprinted in the Smithsonian Annual Report for 1926, gives a detailed account of the making of a double-curved self-bow. According to him, the Omaha did not use the reinforced bow because they considered it relatively weak and easily ruined by rain. There can be no question that the reinforced bow, with its back lined with sinew, was vulnerable to moisture, and this explains why it was confined to the more arid regions of North America; but to say that it was relatively weak when compared with the self-bow is simply contrary to fact, as will be shown in the next chapter.

According to La Flesche's account, among the Omaha the bows were made by specialists, while the bowstrings were made by other specialists and the arrows by still others. Aside from Osage orange, which the Omaha got by trade and valued highly, their preferred bow-woods were ash, white elm and ironwood in that order. The most interesting detail of all was that no tillering whatever was done on the bow itself since the last act of the bowyer, before surrendering the new bow to La Flesche, was to cut the notches for the bowstring. He simply whittled the bow out by eye and had no idea whatever whether it would bend properly when braced. The double-curving was done by greasing the

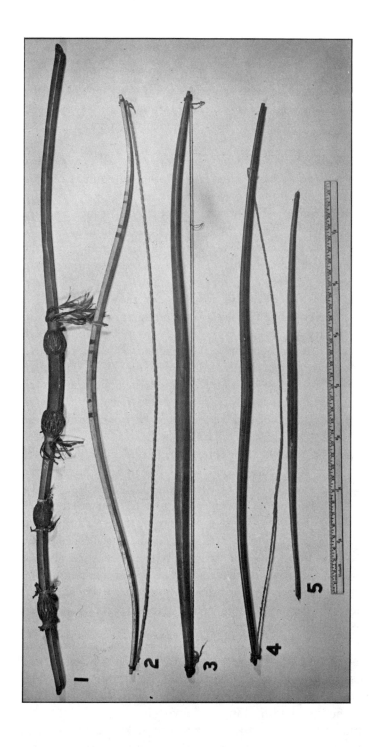

FIGURE 18. Double-curved self-bows of the Plains: (1) Exceptionally powerful Pawnee bow, collected at the Genoa reservation before 1875. Catalogue No. 374. Decorations on the left limb undoubtedly did not improve its performance. (2) Only reflexed double-curved bow yet observed by the author. It has been incorrectly restrung, Catalogue No. 440-40. (3) and (4) Collected by Charley White (Buckskin Charley) in late 1870's or early 1880's, probably from among the Sioux. Catalogue Nos. 2208 and 2207. (5) A boy's D-bow. *Photo courtesy Nebraska State Historical Society.*

"breast" — presumably the back — and then holding the limb over the fire. "When it became hot, he bent it with his foot and held it until it cooled." After receiving the new bow, La Flesche took it to the bowstring maker to be braced and then to the arrow maker to get his arrows.

If this account is accurate — and judging from two self-bows in my own collection, it well could be — then it is a foregone conclusion that Omaha bows were not of much worth, but I imagine that this peculiarity of not tillering their bows was an isolated instance and not true of the tribe as a whole. In any large collection of Plains bows, the majority will always be self-bows, displaying workmanship from the best down to the worst imaginable. The two self-bows mentioned above, which I keep as horrible examples of the bowyer's art, have seen long and hard service; but of what possible use they were to their owners when the going got tough is beyond my imagination.

One other peculiarity of the Plains self-bow should be mentioned. Usually, two notches are used to form the upper nock while only one notch on the left side of the stave forms the lower nock. The reason for this is that the sinew bowstring was tied permanently in the upper nock while the temporary knot or noose fitted into the lower nock. With the notch on only one side, the knot or noose could be worked out of the nock more easily when it was desired to relax the bow.

The problem of the double-curved bow was touched upon in the previous chapter. Just how this peculiar fad became established, or what possible advantage there was in it, is completely baffling. If Le Moyne's sketch is accurate, the practice was not limited to the area west of the Mississippi (Fig. 16). There is, of course, the possibility that Le Moyne was merely exercising artistic license, and introduced some of Cupid's bows into the scene for variety, but, for reasons already mentioned, I believe the bows depicted were in actual use among the Southeastern Indians he saw. The fact that all the bows are relaxed and all of them follow the string, as one would expect self-bows of this length to do, also strengthens my faith in Le Moyne.

This evidence from the Southeast, plus archaeological recoveries of actual double-curved bows or Indian drawings in the Southwest, dating from the 15th Century or earlier, indicates that the double-curving was being practiced over a wide area before the advent of the horse. Thus the shortening of the bow had nothing to do with it.

Anthropologists make much of the fact that in making a bow certain Indians bent, or deformed, one limb more than the other (La Flesche, 1926). Actually, a slight deformation has little effect upon the cast so

46

long as the belly face of the limb does not get behind a line running past the back of the grip. When this occurs in both limbs, as in double-curving, the usual result is a bow which bucks like a bay steer. The Indian bow of Osage, mentioned a few paragraphs back, is a good example.

On the other hand, this bucking of a double-curved bow does not always occur. Recently I was shown a bow by an unknown maker, belonging to a local family and shot in formal archery matches around the year 1880. The bow is of Osage orange, 64-1/2 inches from nock to nock. The grip is plain and unwrapped, oval in cross-section, 1-7/16 x 3/4 inches thick x 7 inches long. At mid-limb the measurement is 1-13/16 x 1/2 inch, and just below the nocks it is 1-1/8 x 3/8 inches. There are a knot in the grip and very small ones in the limbs, and the bow is slightly, but definitely, double-curved. The limbs are a flat oval in cross section.

I made up a string for this bow and tried it out. It had a weight of approximately 50 pounds at 28 inches and cast a 500 grain field arrow 176 yards. *It did not buck.*

Though the family says the grandfather had no contact with Indians of any description, the bow has all the earmarks of having been made by one. To begin with it is a flat bow, which was unheard of among the polite society within which Judge Irvine circulated; they all would have been shooting English longbows. Furthermore, all bowmakers in the English tradition carefully follow the grain on the back and never cut through it indiscriminately as was done on this bow. And, finally, the knots were sanded down flat with the surface and were not raised as is the normal English practice. I might also add that there was no lacquer, or wax finish of any sort. Unfortunately, before it could be determined just why this bow shot better than other double-curved bows, it was returned to the East.

In spite of this experience it still seems that double-curving is a completely useless procedure. The same stave left as a D-bow would shoot equally well, if not better, so why deform the limbs?

Possibly this question should be asked about foot-bows, since there might be some justification for the practice, theoretically at least, in making horse-bows. There can be no question that the big problem in shortening the bow was that of maintaining the draw. Everything else being equal — good bow-wood, good tillering, etc. — as the self-bow is reduced in length so must be the draw, for the working self-bow must maintain a bow-draw ratio of not much less than 2.2 to 1 or it will be in constant danger of breaking. This means then that a D-bow 4 feet long would have a draw just below 22 inches at the very most. If the bow were reduced to 3 feet, the draw could not be over 16 inches and still be reliable.

Double-curving horse-bows might have been an expedient to get around this difficulty by deliberately deforming the limbs until the tips, when relaxed, lay well in front of the grip. Then, when the bow was braced, there would be less initial tension on the limbs at bracing height and a longer draw could be used. It is doubtful whether this would produce any increase in cast, even though a longer draw were possible, because of the loss in initial tension at bracing height. This argument, of course, is mostly based upon theory. Eventually, someone will work out a means of checking the relative merits of the two bows experimentally. If it can be determined why one double-curved bow bucks and another does not, and their relative casts can be compared, we will have gone a long way toward solving the over-all problem.

From the Rio Grande to Terra del Fuego the self-bow was the only known form, except for some reinforced bows carried by an occasional band of Apache or Navajoes in the northern deserts of Mexico. This is not meant to imply that the archery complex of this vast region was or is uncomplicated, for in fact a tremendous variety of bows were used, but we cannot speak too intelligently about the archery of Mexico and South America because of a dearth of printed information. Meyer's study, BOWS AND ARROWS IN CENTRAL BRAZIL (1896), in spite of its title is primarily a study in ethnic relationships. The one great exception is the knowledgeable discussion of bow-making and archery among the Siriono of Eastern Bolivia by Allan R. Holmberg (1950). Another important source of information for this book has been the husband-and-wife team of Clifford Evans and Betty Meggers of the Smithsonian Institution, who have provided valuable photographs as well as their personal observations. Since these three individuals have furnished the most reliable information now available, the archery of the rain forests will receive more attention here than it would if a factual over-all survey could be made.

Metraux (1945:Vol.5:230) makes the statement that the Siriono bows "sometimes measure 12 feet long." Holmberg (1950:145) states that the longest Siriono bow he saw measured 9 feet, 7 inches, while the average bow length was between 7 and 9 feet.

These excessively long bows seem not only to be a characteristic of the Siriono and the rain forests of South America, but of the equatorial belt in Africa as well. They are, in fact, so universal in that latitude that there must be some fundamental but unknown reason for the practice.

Returning to the basic facts of design in a self-bow, efficiency falls off rapidly if the bow-draw ratio rises much above 2.3 to 1. Since these people of the equatorial regions usually tend to be somewhat short in stature, a 28-inch draw is a generous estimate. With a 7-foot bow the bow-draw ratio would be almost 3 to 1, while with a 9-foot bow the ratio would be 4 to 1. The long thick arrows of cane which normally go with these bows would tend to reduce further the efficiency of the cast.

It is really quite a puzzle. Is it perhaps because the natives have not yet discovered a suitable bow-wood, such as lemonwood, *Calycophyllum candidissimum,* known to the lumber trade of that area as degame, and are using instead woods which are too brittle to permit a shorter bow? If lemonwood does not actually grow in the land of the Siriono, surely some closely related and equally suitable wood does. As for the long and heavy arrows, A.V. Kidder once suggested to me that they might possibly be a carry-over from the pre-archery days when the atlatl and dart were in use. No one can deny that the only thing which distinguishes the Colombian arrow, 5 feet long and with tangential fletching, from the ancient atlatl dart is the notch in its butt. Is it possible that the natives adapted the bow to the already existing dart rather than modifying the dart to fit the bow?

Holmberg knows bows as few anthropologists do and his study of Siriono bow-making and shooting is to be highly recommended. Briefly, the bows are made from a variety of the chonta palm, called siris. The outer layer of the palm, about 2 inches thick, is very hard and black; wood from this layer is taken to make the bow, and it is worked before the wood can dry out, usually being scraped down with mollusk shells. The finished bow is roughly oval in cross section; it measures about 2 inches in diameter at the grip and tapers to about 1/4 inch at the tips. There are no notches. The life of a bow is about one year.

"Occasionally, when a hunter notices that his bow is drying out, he places it in water for several nights until its proper resiliency is restored.

"If a hunter is right-handed . . . the bow is drawn in the following manner. It is grasped in the middle with the left hand. Because of its great length, the top horn is tilted at an angle of about 30 degrees to the right of the perpendicular, so that the bottom horn does not rest on the ground. The hunter spaces his feet from 2 to 3 feet apart, the left foot, of course, always being placed forward . . .

"The secondary release is employed in drawing the bow. The arrow is held between the thumb and first finger of the right hand; the remaining fingers assist in drawing the string. The left arm is rigid, and the arrow shaft slides between the thumb and first finger on the side of the bow to the left of the belly. The bow is

FIGURE 19. Yukuma, the Wai Wai hunter with Doctors Evans and Meggers in British Guiana (now Guyana), takes aim on a fish from the prow of a dugout. He is using the fish arrow No. 162 shown in Fig.9A. This is without question one of the best photographs yet made of an Indian archer in action. Yukuma is crouched with his feet out of position. He has the bow almost at full draw and it is cocked at an angle so he can follow the fish. All this is in pleasant contrast to the usual picture of an Eastern or Pueblo Indian in a Plains warbonnet, holding a toy bow. *Courtesy Clifford Evans and Betty Meggers, Smithsonian Institution.*

FIGURE 20.   Yukuma of the Wai Wai in Guyana hunts a fish
in the rapids. This fish is a hard fighter and must be taken
with the harpoon arrow No. 180, shown in Fig. 9A. When the
fish is hit the harpoon head comes off, but is held to the
shaft by the short heavy string. The fish then can be pulled in
without breaking the arrow — if Yukuma can get his hands
on the shaft! *Clifford Evans and Betty Meggers, Smithsonian
Institution.*

drawn to a maximum distance allowed by the arms. As the bowstring passes his head, the hunter sights along the arrow to aim. He withdraws his head just before releasing the arrow, and the string flies by his face" (Holmberg, 1950).

That is one way to lower the bow-draw ratio! The less said about that shooting technique, the better.

The photograph of an Indian shooting fish from the prow of a canoe was taken by Doctors Evans and Meggers while studying the Wai Wai of British Guiana (Fig. 19). This is the best and most authentic photograph I have seen of an American Indian drawing a bow. For some strange reason photographs of native archers are usually made from the back; if from the front, they never manage to catch the shot at full draw. Any man who has ever done any shooting knows instantly that this is a picture of the real thing; there is nothing posed or artificial about it.

In response to some questions about this photograph, Doctors Evans and Meggers kindly supplied the following additional information:

"We have gone through our specimens and notes, and extracted the following information:

"1) Two pictures are enclosed of close-up shots showing the method of pull. As best we could determine the grip is the most common one. The length of pull [draw] was always about this complete [Fig. 21].

"2) We measured . . . the force of pull [weight] of the bow we brought back which is the exact duplicate of Yukuma's. Your guess of around 40 pounds is quite close . . . However, . . . we did not quite reach the full draw of the bow, or the 28" you mentioned.

"3) The length of the arrows as shown in the pictures is quite typical, but we measured them and here is the information. Both the two-barbed, and the many barbed types for shooting small animals such as agouti, coati, monkey, etc., measure the following lengths: 197 cm., 198.5 cm., and 175 cm. [78 - 68 inches]. The weight of each of these was 2-1/2 ounces.

"4) The poison arrow for shooting monkeys weighed 2-1/2 ounces, and measured 206.5 cm. long [81 inches].

"5) The arrow used by the Wai Wai for shooting fish from the prow of the dugout as illustrated in the article [Fig. 19] weighs 2-1/4 ounces and measures 181 cm. long [72 inches].

"6) The spear arrow with a wide metal blade for shooting tapir measures 198 cm. long [78 inches].

"In other words, they all run approximately the same length with only slight variations, but are made in two sections. A pithy reed is the main shaft measuring from 164 to 178 cm. [64 - 68 inches]. The points make up the rest of the length and are usually made of a hard wood or split cane with poison added for monkeys,

FIGURE 21. The Wai Wai draw, utilizing the Tertiary. These Indians of British Guiana place the arrow on the left side of the bow. Note the extremely high bow-draw ratio. *Clifford Evans and Betty Meggers, Smithsonian Institution.*

but since the advent of trade with Europeans, metal points sometimes appear. This reed makes them much lighter than you predict . . . for they all appear to run around 2 to 2-1/2 ounces maximum, due to the light weight of the pithy reed.

"7) A few comments about the bow. It is made from a special hard wood [letter wood — *Brosimum aublettii*] found in the headwaters of the Mapuera River and is not common in British Guiana. The bows all average over 6 feet, and usually over 7 feet. The one we measured now in the United States National Museum, which we collected from the Wai Wai, is 2.245 meters, which converts roughly to 88-3/8″. Its cross section is shown in a sketch in the margin. [Same as English longbow.] A child's bow made from a broken full size bow of the same wood was 95.3 cm. [approximately 37.5 inches] long and gave a 9 pound pull. For the smaller child's bow they make a proportionately shorter arrow.

"8) They do not use a shorter arrow for any purpose whatsoever . . . [It] is generally considered that the Indians claim they go straighter through the heavy brush in the treetops when they are long. This, of course, might be a non-practical explanation . . .

"It has been seen by us and Holmberg, that the Indian will not shoot unless he is positively guaranteed a hit. The reason for this is that they are such successful imitators of bird and animal calls, that they will actually bring the bird or animal within 10 or 25 feet, if at all possible. About the longest range would be the shooting of monkeys in the treetops."

By far the greater number of arrowheads from this region are of wood. The region abounds in hardwoods which are true to their name and make excellent and serviceable points, and certain types of cane are also well fitted to the purpose.

The various types of arrowheads of the Wai Wai, as observed and illustrated by Evans and Meggers, are of particular interest because of the functional foreshaft points (Fig. 9). In every instance where solid wood has been inserted into the reed shaft, it has been done with the immediate intent of arming the arrow. There is some hint of the foreshaft in arrow No. 161, but it is primarily a point.

Arrowheads from Colombia, a thousand or more miles from the land of the Wai Wai, have a very definite difference in basic design (Fig. 22). Because of the iron points, the foreshafts play a distinctly secondary role. Furthermore, the elaborate carving does not alter the fact that they are rather unnecessary. Undoubtedly, some barbs on the foreshafts are helpful in holding the game, but with these arrows the only barbs which will be effective are those on the arrow with the smallest point. The iron arrowheads on the first two arrows are too wide to allow the barbs on the foreshafts to hold. Therefore, they are non-functional.

It is interesting to note that Indians using modern iron arrowheads would still be so tradition-ridden that they continue to lavish long

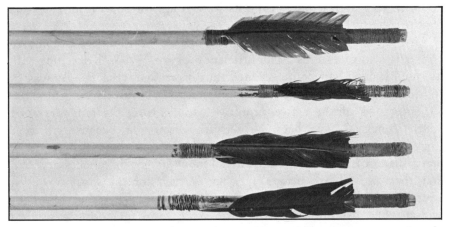

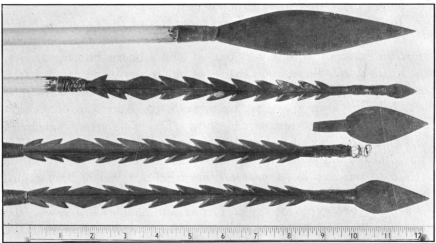

FIGURE 22. Nock and head ends of four Colombian arrows. Note the tangential fletching. The arrows, from top to bottom, weigh respectively 3.1, 1.5, 2.5 and 2.3 ounces. The detached arrowhead weighs 15 grams, or slightly over a half-ounce. All four arrows are approximately 60 inches long. *The Robert S. Waggoner collection, Marshall, Mo. Photos by the author.*

hours carving useless barbs on a uselessly long foreshaft after any need for those barbs has disappeared.

An examination of the fletching on the Wai Wai and the Colombian arrows is also of interest. The efficiency of the Wai Wai fletching with its spiral lashing can be questioned, but it is radial (Fig. 9). By way of contrast, the fletching on the Colombian arrows is strictly tangential.

The arrows of these two primitive peoples from the rain forests of South America have been chosen for discussion because of their contrasts and similarities. They are similar in that they all have arrow shafts made of reeds, that they are all much longer than necessary, and that they are all exceptionally heavy — even for the most powerful bows. The Wai Wai arrows run between 72 and 81 inches in length over-all. The Colombian arrows are much more uniform, measuring from 59-3/4 inches to 61 inches in length over-all.

As for weight, the Wai Wai arrows range from 2 to 2.5 ounces; while the Colombian arrows weigh 2.3, 2.5, 1.5 and 3.1 ounces respectively.

For purposes of comparison one of our modern hunting arrows, armed with a broadhead and capable of killing any game native to the Western Hemisphere, seldom weighs more than 1.25 ounces, or just about half the average weight of these South American projectiles. Furthermore, the iron arrowhead shown beside its arrow weighs 15 grams (Fig. 22). One of our modern three-blade broadheads weighs 7.5 grams, and the only Old English broadhead (Currelly; 1939) which has survived to our day in its near original condition weighs 9.65 grams. The relative inefficiency of the long Indian arrows should be obvious.

When the two types of Indian arrows are compared, one with the other, the Wai Wai shows considerably more sophistication than the Colombian. Actually, if the foreshafts on the Colombian arrows were set loose in the reed arrow shafts and a cup substituted for the notch in the nock, there would be nothing except the iron points to distinguish them from the ancient darts thrown with the atlatl.

In Terra del Fuego, the extreme southern tip of South America, where conditions are entirely different from those in the rain forests, we find the Onas with a most interesting bow. Bridges (1949:376-9) describes both the bow and the arrow in detail. His description may be summarized as follows:

1. The Ona bow was about 4-1/2 feet in length.
2. The arrow was carefully made and barreled in shape, 1/3 inch in diameter tapering to 1/6 inch at each end. The length was approximately 30 inches. The draw is not given, but, because of the bow length,

could not have been more than 24 inches, and the bow could not have been very powerful with the ends of the arrow tapered down to 1/6 inch. Bow weight probably would have been about 50 pounds at 24 inches.

3. The arrow was tangentially fletched with two feathers about 2 inches long.

4. The Secondary release was used.

5. The stone point, measuring 1 x 1/2 inches, would weigh approximately 1 gram.

It seems logical to conclude that the Ona had an archery adequate to their environment before the advent of the white man.

Another puzzle of South American native archery is the failure of the Indians of the Pampas, who took to the horse as readily as did the Plains Indians of North America, to modify the bow for use on horseback. Metraux (1945:Vol.5) states that "Unlike North American Indians, the equestrian tribes of the Pampas did not modify their bow so that it could be used on horseback . . . The bow survived among Chaco horsemen, but they employed it only when they hunted or fought on foot." As will be seen in the next chapter, the Plains Indians of North America solved this problem of modification brilliantly with the reinforced bow.

4

The Reinforced Bow

There are a large number of reinforced bows in museum collections. These relatively modern bows fall into two main classifications: the reinforced Plains bow and the California bow. Both are built upon the same principles, but the bows themselves are quite different in appearance as well as performance, since the former was made for use on horseback and the latter on foot.

Three features distinguish the reinforced bow from all others: (1) it is built upon a wooden stave; (2) the back of the stave is lined with a thin sheet of sinew securely glued down, and (3) the bow is always reflexed.

The Reinforced Plains Bow. The better examples of the reinforced Plains bow are so uniform in design they can almost be considered a standardized product. I have three in my own small collection: two collected from the Apache in the Southwest and one from among the Dakotah on the Northern high Plains. The two better examples are almost identical in every respect except that the Apache bow is built on a white oak stave and the Dakotah on one of juniper. Also, the Apache bow displays better workmanship — it was made by a very careful and meticulous bowyer — but the bows themselves were probably about equal in cast. As is usually the case with working bows, they are practically without decoration. I do not think that the "Apache" bow was necessarily made by an Apache nor the "Dakotah" by a Dakotah, for this uniformity in design was probably due to intertribal trading and the fighting which was going on constantly. Enemy bows were picked up after a skirmish, used, and, if of better design, copied.

A description of my Apache bow will serve as well as any in identifying the type. This weapon is 44-1/2 inches long over-all, and 43-1/2 inches between the nocks, which, in each instance, are two notches cut into the sides of the stave. The stave is of white oak, rectangular in cross section. The center of the grip is 22 inches from the upper tip and measures 1-5/32 x 3/4 inches. Eleven inches from the two tips the limb measures 1-1/32 x 5/8 inches; one inch below the upper nock the measurement is 11/16 x 1/2 inches, and one inch above the lower nock it measures 11/16 x 17/32 of an inch.

The sinew backing, or lining, appears to be about 1/16 inch in thickness, but it may be greater toward the center since the back of the bow is slightly rounded. The backing goes over the tips and down on the belly side to the nocks where it is whipped down with sinew thread. Other whipping is applied here and there at points where the maker felt the backing might come loose. The sinew backing is extremely hard and looks like the bark on a young hickory sapling.

The reflex, measured from the back of the grip to a straight line drawn from tip to tip, is 5-3/8 inches.

There are, of course, variations. These bows seldom have notches; the nocks usually being formed by wrapping sinew thread about an inch below the tips until a ridge is formed against which the bowstring can rest. The belly is usually flat, and the back and sides can be square across or rounded, but the better examples are between 42 and 45 inches in length and they have a reflex of 5 to 7 inches which has been maintained with little or no deformation.

Technically, the sheet of sinew glued to the back is called a "backing," but I prefer to use the term "lining" to distinguish between this type of bow and the American composite, or horn bow, which is a "sinew-*back*." "Sinew-back*ed*" and "sinew-*back*" are quite correct as distinguishing terms, but lead to confusion.

As it is, our anthropologists invariably refer to these reinforced bows as "double-curved," whereas the double-curved bow is almost without exception a self-bow. They assume that the reflex is merely a badly warped double-curved bow. For example, Wissler (1901: 155-6) makes this error in reference to his Figure 101: an excellent example of a fine reinforced Plains bow which has reversed itself in the string during the years it has lain in storage. The drawing even shows the bowstring still knotted on the belly side, but now twisted and running along the back.

The bow previously described has done the same thing. As explained in Chapter I, when braced the reinforced bow does have an outline similar to the double-curve, but there all similarities cease. The double-curve is essentially stable since the Cupid's bow outline is due to deforming the limbs, but the reinforced bow is kept in that outline only by the tension on the bowstring. If it is not relaxed when put in storage, it will continue straining until the string stretches to the point where the bow can reverse itself. When the wood and sinew of the bow become permanently set before the string stretches enough to permit the reverse, then we have what appears at first glance to be a true double-curved sinew-lined bow, but it is merely a reinforced bow which has given up the struggle. Again, the suggestion of double-curving sometimes seen in relaxed reinforced bows is due to the weapon having been put into service before the wood was properly seasoned, or because the sinew backing was too heavy, causing the wooden stave in the belly to follow the string.

The outstanding feature about these reinforced bows, when in the relaxed state, is that so many of them still retain a perfect reflex even though they carry the unmistakable signs of hard usage. One would expect the wood cells on the belly side to show some sign of collapsing – some tendency to follow the string – as they invariably do in self-bows of the Plains type.

I have puzzled over the ability of the reinforced bow to hold its reflex ever since realizing that I was working with a distinctly different type. Fortunately, Dale Henning, at that time director of archaeology, University of Missouri, discussed the question of identifying the wood used in native bows with Robert C. Koeppen, plant taxonomist in wood identification at the National Woods Products Laboratory, Madison, Wisconsin, and Koeppen offered to identify the wood in any bows we cared to submit. Consequently, Dr. Henning took my collection with him the next time he drove to Madison. When Koeppen's report (No Date) came in it was astonishing to learn that of my three reinforced Plains bows, two were built on white oak staves and one on juniper, since it had been assumed that the two were on black locust staves and the third on red cedar. Oak, because of the extreme flexibility required in the draw on these short bows, had not occurred to me, and certainly not juniper for it is an exceedingly soft and easily deformed wood.

I next asked Koeppen if he would please check the maximum crushing strength of certain bow-woods. This was done and the results were as follows (Koeppen, 1965. Bendtsen, 1966):

	Pounds Per Square Inch
Eastern Red Cedar *(Juniperus virginiana)*	6,020
White Oak *(Quercus alba)*	7,440
Black Locust *(Robinia pseudoacacia)*	10,800
Osage Orange *(Maclura pomifera)*	9,800
Pacific Yew *(Taxus brevifolia)*	9,220
Rocky Mountain Juniper *(Juniperus scopularium)*	4,220 (estimate)

The last wood listed could not be tested for lack of a sample, but its strength was estimated to be approximately the same as that of the alligator juniper of Southeastern United States, *Juniperus pachyphloea.*

It is interesting to note that Pacific yew is almost as strong as Osage orange; this explains why it does not follow the string in a self-bow as does the English yew. One would expect that the California bow would be made primarily from yew, but Pope, in his excellent study, YAHI ARCHERY (1918: 106) observes that Ishi apparently used only juniper before he was captured and brought to the museum to live. Since juniper can be used successfully on the California reinforced bows as well as on those of the Plains type, the only possible answer is that in some way the sinew backing shifts the stresses within the limb, when the bow is brought to full draw, in such a way as to enable the wooden belly to support the load without having the cells collapse.

In this connection, the reversed Apache bow which was described has a slight deformation in the *lower* limb, but it is not enough to affect its shooting qualities. It also has two knots in the wood stave: one in the grip and a second about four inches from the grip in the *upper* limb. This is mentioned to emphasize that, though there is now a break in this second knot, the limb itself is not at all deformed. What deformation there is is in the lower limb where there is no flaw in the wood.

The question is, why would an expert bowmaker, such as the one who made that bow, lavish all that care and work in making a bow with a faulty stave? One day when showing the bow to a visitor I noticed that the break in the knot was a tension break and not from compression: the wood fibers, torn loose at the surface of the belly, showed plainly that the bow had been broken by someone pulling backward on the string *after the bow had reversed itself*. It has broken from abuse, not use.

This indicated that the old bowyer had known that knots in the stave of a reinforced bow were not so serious a defect as I had assumed. If the knots were not a serious defect in a reinforced bow, it must mean that the entire wooden stave was under compression from belly to back when brought to full draw, and that the tensile stresses had been shifted into the sinew backing, or lining. If the plane of neutral tension had been shifted to the back of the wooden stave, it followed that the load-carrying capacity of the stave had been doubled and that was why the wood cells in the belly of a reflexed sinew-lined bow did not collapse and follow the string, as they did in a self-bow.

This innovation in bow design raises many interesting speculations. Where and how did the primitive bowmakers first find that sinew could be used so effectively in giving cast to a bow? Was it a chance discovery after first applying sinew to the back of a self-bow in an attempt to prevent the grain of the wood from feathering up, or was it logically reasoned out? If they reasoned it out, how did they know that dry sinew stretches and has such a quick recovery? Are we seeing here an independent American development in bow design, completely divorced from Asia, or was the concept of the reinforced bow introduced in some way from there? If so, how? Did the bowmakers know why the wooden stave did not follow the string, or merely that it did not when backed with a certain amount of sinew? Did they know what proportions to use, or was the application of the sinew a hit-or-miss process?

It is known that the reinforced bow, as defined here, was widely used throughout Asia and Europe, but not in Africa. The forms these bows took, however, were not at all similar to anything made in the Western Hemisphere. Luschan (1899, Figs. 4, 4a) illustrated one, presumably from the Bashkir, a people who formerly lived in the area around present-day Magnitogorsk, U.S.S.R. His illustration is reproduced here (Fig. 23). At the time he wrote, this ancient relic was in the museum in Braunschweig, Germany, and in very bad repair. Adler (1902) also mentions various reinforced bows, but his illustrator shows none of these in cross section. Most of the questions raised above must await further research before there can even be an attempt to guess the answers.

I have been unable to find a good description of the making of a reinforced Plains bow. The critical question is, how did the makers induce the reflex? Did they deliberately deform the limbs with heat, or did they depend upon the contraction of the drying sinew to pull the stave into the reflex? I suspect it was a combination of the two, but, in any event, it took great skill to get just the correct set to the limbs. The Havasupai were not Plains Indians, nor were their bows Plains bows, but Spier (1928: 148) gives some useful information which may apply. Note that the Havasupai gave their bows about the same length — five spans, or 40 to 45 inches — but they reduced the thickness of the stave by one-half. Oak so thin will not take that load without following the string. I have a Plains bow with sinew lining 1/4 inch thick on an oak stave measuring 19/32 of an inch and it is badly deformed.

"Oak is used as well as ash for the sinew-backed bows: it is grown the same way. Mesquite is also used, if it contains a dark streak. The bow resembles the self bow, but is somewhat shorter, five spans and only half as thick, although the width is the same. After seasoning two months or more until it is thoroughly dry, it is ready for the sinew reinforcement. Nocks are first cut. The back is scraped as smooth as

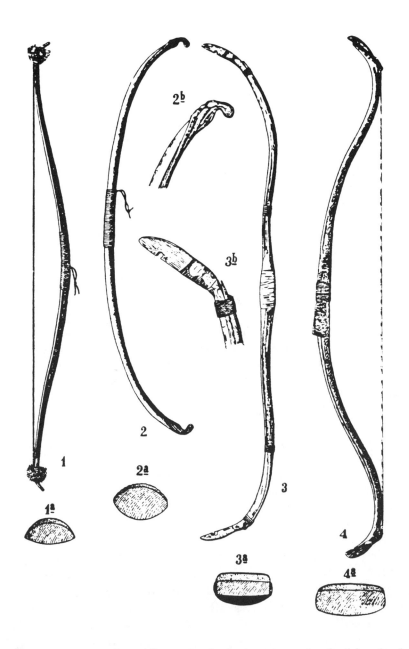

FIGURE 23. A page from Felix von Luschan's pioneering study of reinforced and composite bows, written in 1899. Nos. 1 and 2 are California bows braced and relaxed, with the cross sections of wood and sinew shown below. No. 3 is a composite bow made by a people formerly living at the south end of the Ural Mountains near where Magnitogorsk, U.S.S.R., now stands. Note the siyah or "ear" in 3b as compared with 2b. No. 4 is a reinforced bow thought to have come from the same area. At the time Luschan wrote, this bow was in the Braunschweig Museum in Germany, in poor condition. The principle of the reinforced bow was widely used throughout Asia as well as the western half of North America.

possible and fine lines are scratched on it longitudinally, using a flat flake with a serrated edge. After glue is applied over half the back, a broad sinew is laid on beginning at the middle, stretching it toward the tip. This is rubbed in the same direction with a smooth stick in order to make it adhere. The process is repeated for the other half of the bow, the sinew layers lapping in the middle. Three more layers are similarly added, setting the bow in the sun to dry partially before each application. The sinew extends over the back quite to the inner face. The first two layers are brought over each end and down the face for about 1 cm. The ends of the last two layers are left free, but twisted together. A sinew is bound in the nocks to hold the sinew backing fast . . ."

Pope's (1923:342) findings on the performance of a sinew-backed reflexed Plains bow are particularly appropriate at this point.

"This bow has seen considerable service, and bears evidence of many greasings and hard use. It is a piece of split hickory, heavily backed with sinew, with short rounded nocks. Length, 40 inches; diameter below the handgrip is 1-3/8 by 5/8, circumference 3-1/4 inches; at mid-limb it is 1-1/4 by 1/2, circumference, 3 inches; below the nock, 3/4 by 1/2, circumference, 2 inches. On cross section it is lenticular, or a flat oval. The sinew draws it into a reflexed position when not braced. The string is made of two strands of twisted sinew, having a slipknot at the upper nock, and half-hitches at the lower. When braced it is a springy, vigorous weapon, and by far the best shooter in the group. When drawn 20 inches it weighs 40 pounds and shoots 153 yards.

"It is possible that in its youth this Blackfoot bow might have been drawn farther and have shot harder, but now it cracks ominously when drawn above 20 inches. This seems to be the type of weapon that was used on horseback and doubtless it is strong enough for buffalo hunting. Mr. Jessop [the owner] assures me that it is a buffalo bow. If this be the case we must assume that it does not take a very powerful weapon to kill bison."

Pope does not appear to be greatly impressed with the performance of this little bow, but a cast of 153 yards with a draw of only 20 inches at 40 pounds is impressive indeed! Also, to have been able to draw an ancient 40-inch bow 20 inches after it had lain for years in the superheated attic of a museum speaks well for the man who made it. That is a 2 to 1 ratio and is most probably the ratio at which it worked in its buffalo-hunting days.

Obviously, a 40-inch reinforced bow with a 20-inch draw and a cast of 153 yards at 100 years of age did not come into being overnight. Strangely enough, its ancestor can be identified in the accounts of the Spanish explorers in the Southwest during the 16th Century. The first possible reference to them appears to have been made by Cabeza de

Vaca (1542), who says, as a result of difficulties he had in saving his Indian friends from slavery after they had delivered him to his Christian compatriots:

"In consequence of the dispute, we left at our departure many bows of Turkish shape we had along with us . . ."

Though many other indefinite references to bows appear in the succeeding years, it is not until the period between 1582 and 1598 that the term "Turkish" is again used.

Diego Perez de Luxan in his JOURNAL OF THE EXPEDITION INTO NEW MEXICO MADE BY ANTONIA DE ESPEJO, 1582-1583 (Hammond and Rey, 1929, p. 57) reports on some Otomoacos Indians living a few miles above the mouth of the Conchos River where it joins the Rio Grande, saying that "The bows are Turkish, all reinforced and very strong, and the strings are made from the sinews of the buffalo." Later on their return journey he observes that the Abriaches Indians at the junction of the Conchos and Rio Grande traded them "blankets, of which they had many, bison skins, and Turkish bows reinforced with sinews. These are the best and the strongest which there are in the land that has been discovered" (page 126).

Apparently not all of these "Turkish bows" were reinforced or very powerful, for when Espejo reached the Piro Pueblos, Luxan (page 74) reports that "They have few and poor Turkish bows and arrows." Other observations are equally conflicting and equally puzzling, regardless of the chronicler. Actually, of the lot, Luxan is the only one who furnishes any detail whatever. Near present El Paso he further reports (page 69) that the Tanpachoas "fight with Turkish bows . . . made of tornillo wood [screw bean mesquite], which is strong and flexible."

Since these "Turkish bows" which won his respect were in different locations — El Paso being about 200 airline miles upstream from the mouth of the Conchos — there is no way to say positively that the ones reinforced with sinew were also made of mesquite. But because this is all essentially the same type of desert, it is probable that they were, for the very practical reason that mesquite is the best type of bow-wood growing in that immediate area. Therefore as unsatisfactory as these descriptions are, a reasonably accurate idea can be gained of just what these early Spanish observers saw by combining their key words "Turkish bows reinforced with sinews . . . made of Tornillo wood, which is strong and flexible." They are here obviously speaking of the wooden, reflexed, sinew-lined bow, also known as the reinforced. When braced, it assumed the Cupid's bow outline which they had seen in the composites carried by the Moors and known superficially to the Spaniards as the "Turkish bow."

This indicates then that, along the Rio Grande at least, certain groups of Indians had developed bow making to a rather advanced stage by 1582, while others farther up the river, at the Piro Pueblos, for instance, were using weak, double-curved self-bows, which the uncritical Luxan also called "Turkish." A connection of some sort seems to exist between the powerful reflexed bows of the Rio Grande observed by Luxan in 1582 and "very large Turkish bows" reported by Onate as being used by the foot Indians on the Plains in 1598 (Hammond and Rey, 1953, p. 404). That appears to be all the useful information on bows which can be extracted from the early Spanish sources.

The modification of the "very large Turkish bows" of the Plains Indians, as they hunted the buffalo on foot in 1582, into the compact 40-inch buffalo bow tested by Pope probably took place within one generation after the advent of the horse. Once it was realized that a less powerful bow could still make the kill, if released at point-blank range, any competent bowmaker could reduce the length in conformity with the shorter draw.

The Plains arrows in my collection permit draws from 20 to 23 inches, so it can be safely assumed that these bows were designed for not over 23 inches. It would be desirable to brace these bows and see what their actual draw and weight is, but respect for their age prohibits that. The weight of these bows might be estimated in the neighborhood of 70 pounds at 23 inches; about all any man on a galloping pony could draw and still stay aboard.

The most plausible eyewitness of the power of the reinforced bow is Captain J.C. Bourke, an American officer who saw much service against the Apache, and who at one time determined how long it would take Indians, completely deprived of weapons, to rearm themselves by allowing some captive Apache to do just that while he remained in the background and watched. Bourke commented (Leeper, 1897: 201) that once he was ambushed by the Apache and two of their arrows drove into pine trees "to a depth of at least six inches. The distance we were from the Indians on the Hay Fork was stepped the next day and found to be 250 paces, though the arrows had been elevated and discharged from a position considerably above us."

With all due respect to Captain Bourke, I find the arrows sunk six inches into a pine tree hard to believe. Apparently he did too, since he goes on to explain it was a down shot, so the arrows still had plenty of drive when they struck. Assuming that their pace equaled 28 inches, the distance shot was approximately 195 yards. Undoubtedly the Apache were using reinforced bows, for there is no evidence of their having American composites.

The California Bow. There were many interesting bow types on the Pacific Coast during the early historic period, but little specific information is to be found among the writings of the explorers. Drake, with archers of his own aboard the Golden Hind as she lay in a bay on the California coast in 1579, was definitely unimpressed with the aboriginal archery. In his report, THE WORLD ENCOMPASSED, he observes that

". . . Their bowes and arrowes (their only weapons, and almost all their wealth) they use very skillfully, but yet not to do any great harm with them, being by reason of their weakness more fit for children than for men, sending the arrowes neither farre off nor with any great force . . ."

Not all native bows were so contemptible. A German named Meyer, in his book NACH DEM SACRAMENTO, mentions briefly a bow which even the Old English might have spoken of with respect. After discussing short bows, 3-1/2 feet long and backed with bear's sinew, which apparently were similar to a type that will be described in a moment, he goes on to speak of a much more powerful weapon used for "distance shooting." His description reads:

". . . Still bigger bows [are made] which serve them for distance shooting. These are 6 feet long, and the Indians lie down upon the ground to brace them by thrusting their right knee into the bow and drawing it to them with both arms."

The bow type with which this chapter is concerned bears no similarity whatever to these longbows. For want of a better name, we will call it the California bow since its center, during the historic period, has been about the San Francisco Bay area and north along the coast to the locale of the Hupa and Yurok Indians. Variants of this type are found as far east as the Lake Tahoe region near the present Nevada border, which was inhabited then by the Washo Indians.

These California bows are as short as 32 inches, but 42 inches seems to be an average length. They are lenticular in cross section; at mid-limb the width is at least three times the thickness and usually about four. Either yew or juniper is used, and they are lined with sinew. And last, but far from least, they are heavily reflexed. If a bow has those three characteristics — lenticular in cross section, sinew-lined, and reflexed — then it is a good example of the type here under discussion.

In NORTH AMERICAN BOWS, ARROWS AND QUIVERS (1893), Mason illustrates a Hupa bow of the California type. In this instance the degree of reflex shown is much less pronounced than many of the examples to be seen in various collections. Mason (1886) also quotes Ray, who lived among the Hupa, on the making of these weapons:

"To make a bow, the wood of a yew sapling 2-1/2 to 3 inches in diameter is selected and rough hewn to shape, the heart side inward and the back carefully smoothed to form the back of the bow. The sinew is laid on while the wood is green, and held in place until dry by means of a twine wrapping. In this condition it is hung in the sweat-house until the wood is thoroughly seasoned, when it is finished and strung, and in some cases the back is varnished and painted. The most delicate part of the operation is to get the proper tension on the sinew backing. If too tight the wood crimps or splinters when the bow is strung, and a lack of proper tension leaves the bow weak and worthless. When the bow is seasoned it has a reverse [reflex] curve of about 3 inches.

"The sinew for the backing and bowstring is taken from the back and hind leg of the deer at the time of killing, and dried for future use. When required it is soaked and laid on by commencing at each end and terminating at the center of the bow. The sinew is slightly twisted and dried before it is placed on the bow."

The California bow was not particularly powerful. Ray, again quoted by Mason (1886), has observed its performance in the field.

"The bows are effective for game up to 50 to 75 yards, and will inflict a serious wound at 100 yards. At 50 yards the arrows will penetrate a deer 5 to 10 inches. I never heard of one passing entirely through a deer."

The best comparative information we have on California bow performances are those recorded by Saxton Pope (1923) at the University of California and published in reports of the University Press. The Indian, Ishi, through whom Pope (1918: 125) first became interested in archery, was asked to select for testing the bow which he considered to be the best in the University Museum. He chose a Yurok bow, weighing about 40 pounds at 25 inches, heavily backed with sinew and similar to those of his own manufacture. It was warmed carefully before bracing, but Ishi shot only 175 yards in spite of using a light flight arrow.

68

Other bows of this type, tested by Pope, had the following casts:

	Draw	Weight	Cast
Hupa	22 inches	40 pounds	148 yards
Yurok	28 inches	30 pounds	140 yards
Yana	28 inches	48 pounds	205 yards

All these shots were made using the same flight arrow. Arrows of native manufacture would have been about 75 percent as effective.

From Ray's description just given, as well as Pope's (1918: 107) observations, it is evident that the reflex in these bows was the result of the drying out of the sinew on the back, and not of deliberately tying the limbs backward before the sinew was applied. The amount of sinew used must have been in some proportion to the length of the bow and the thickness of the wood for, as the sinew backing, or lining, dried, it shrank and drew the bow stave into the reflex. That is what Ray meant when he said that the "most delicate part of the operation is in getting the proper tension on the sinew backing."

It is interesting to note that Pope (page 108) states that the bowstring had a loop, and he describes Ishi's difficulties in making a loop which would hold properly. Pope (page 109) records that Ishi in shooting a 45-inch bow used a draw of 25 inches. That is an astounding 1.8 to 1 bow-draw ratio.

These California bows, as a class, excite the admiration of anyone who has ever made a successful self-bow. Not all of them are as large as the Yahi or Yurok, but they are as beautifully made. There are four Washo bows in the collection of the Chicago Museum of Natural History which measure from 34 to 37 inches from nock to nock. They appear to be of yew, lined with sinew and all excellently tillered. The sinew strings all have loops. In this same collection is a Washo arrow (catalogue No. 58370) which is especially noteworthy. It is an outstanding example of native arrow-making at its best. The shaft is only 24-1/2 inches long and 5/16 inches in diameter. The foreshaft is 5-1/4 inches in length and armed with an obsidian point 1-1/4 x 1/4 with side notching. The three feathers, radially mounted, are 5 inches long.

5

The Eskimo Bow and the Asiatic Composite

In order to understand the American composite and its significance in the evolution of the bow in the Western Hemisphere it will be necessary to take up first the problem of the Eskimo bow and the Asiatic weapon from which it was derived. There is nothing new nor startling in pointing out this relationship, for more than eighty years ago General Pitt-Rivers, in his comments appended to Balfour's (1889: 247) classic paper, ON THE STRUCTURE AND AFFINITIES OF THE COMPOSITE BOW, reiterated two of his hypotheses which have been generally accepted by all who have followed:

(1) "That it probably originated through necessity in a region in which suitable elastic woods for the plain [self] bow were not to be procured," and that (2) "the connection between the Chinese bow and the bow of the Western Esquimaux is rendered certain by the adoption in both of the curved back straight pieces at the ends, which Mr. Balfour terms 'ears', . . . the particular use of which is not very clear."

To these hypotheses the General added a third, which appears somewhat more questionable, "that the Esquimaux bow . . . presented the survival of the earliest form of the composite."

Not only Balfour, but Luschan (1899) in his ZUSAMMENGE-SETZTE UND VERSTAERKTE BOGEN, and Adler (1902) in DIE BOGEN NORDASIENS accepted the first two hypotheses as more or less self-evident. Adler repeated Pitt-Rivers' third hypothesis concerning the invention of the composite in the North, but held in greater favor still another suggestion of the General that it had possibly originated in some desert area in the South of Asia. All three agreed that the composite undoubtedly came into being as a substitute weapon because of the scarcity of good bow-wood for the making of self-bows.

In reading these papers written almost three-quarters of a century ago, one is impressed with the keen insight exhibited by their authors in spite of the lack of basic information at that time. Pitt-Rivers' statement that he did not understand the "particular use" of the "ears" and his assumption (p. 249) that "the composite bow does not appear

70

to be superior, but, if anything, an inferior weapon to the plain [self] bow" are cases in point. But he was writing ten years before Luschan presented his remarkably perceptive study and thirty-six years before Hein (1925-26) published his classic BOGENHANDWERK UND BOGENSPORT BEI DEN OSMANEN (Bowmaking and Flight Shooting among the Ottomen) which made the works of Mustafa Kani, the Turkish master of the composite, available to the West. As a result, the function of the "ears," or siyahs, is well known today and no one can question the superiority of a type of bow which still holds the world record of shooting an arrow 972 yards (Klopsteg, 1927: 24)!

In the light of these developments, it shall be my purpose to show how the Eskimo bow is not only related to, but derived or modified from the Asiatic composite. I shall also show how certain archaeological discoveries during the past few years impinge upon the other hypotheses of General Pitt-Rivers — the Northern and Southern Asiatic origins of the composite concept.

This discussion will be based upon the evidence to be found in the details of construction exhibited by the two varieties of bows. So that my argument can be followed intelligently it will be necessary first to define the Asiatic composite, describe its basic construction, and discuss in some detail the function of the siyahs — the "ears" which so puzzled the General.

Unlike the self-bow, the composite is a highly complex weapon. In its most elementary form it consists of a belly made from horn or antler to which is glued a back of sinew. The thickness of the horn and sinew layers is approximately the same. The American horn bow is an example. The Asiatic composite reflects millenia of experiment and development. It always has a wooden core or foundation strip, to the opposite sides of which are glued the horn belly and the sinew back (Fig. 24).

Each of these materials, the horn and the sinew, can be subjected to much greater stresses of compression and tension respectively than can the best of bow-woods. Consequently the better examples of the composite could be made much shorter in relationship to the length of the draw, with corresponding increases in efficiency and cast.

In addition to the horn belly and the sinew back, another characteristic of the composite is the "reflex." Some of the Asiatic composites, such as the Turkish and the Korean, were so highly reflexed that their outlines, when relaxed and viewed from the side, look like the capital letter "C" (Fig. 25). As has been shown in previous

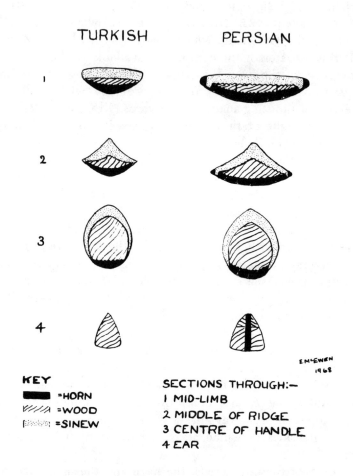

TURKISH   PERSIAN

1

2

3

4

E.M^cEWEN
1968

KEY

■ =HORN

⧄⧄⧄ =WOOD

▒ =SINEW

SECTIONS THROUGH:—
1 MID-LIMB
2 MIDDLE OF RIDGE
3 CENTRE OF HANDLE
4 EAR

FIGURE 24. Representative cross sections of Asiatic composite bows. The "ridge" or knee is the portion of the arm where it merges with the siyah, or "ear." *Redrawn by Edward McEwen after Hein (1925-26) with minor modifications based on personal observation.*

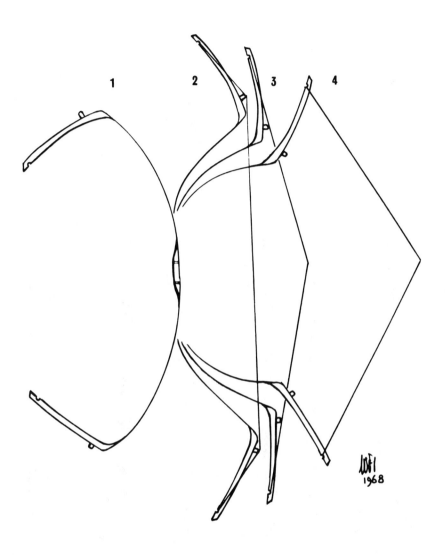

1   2   3   4

FIGURE 25. Schematic drawing of a Sino-Tartar bow: (1) relaxed; (2) braced; (3) as the bowstring lifts off the bridges, and (4) at full draw. *By William F. Paterson.*

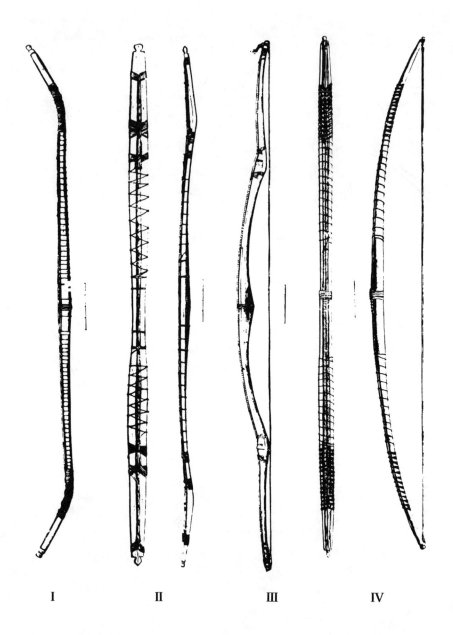

I II III IV

FIGURE 26. The four basic types of Eskimo bows: (I) with functional siyahs; (II) with vestigial siyahs; (III) a confused pattern where the siyahs are usually non-functional, and (IV) the final mature form, perfectly adapted to the Arctic environment. Back views of II and IV are also shown. In all side views the back of the bow is to the left. *Drawings from Murdoch (1884), Plates IV, VII, III and IV respectively.*

chapters, not all reflexed bows are composites, but all true composites are reflexed.

In the Eskimo bow the wood has little elasticity but it serves a double purpose: it forms the skeleton or structural framework and it also acts as the belly half of the bow arm. As in the reinforced bow, this wooden belly takes the compressive stresses imposed by the elaborate network of sinew cables which form the back and provide the cast (Figs. 26 and 27).. Though the Eskimos used antler or bone only when suitable wood was not available, their bow was built strictly upon the composite principle and it should be considered a modified form of that type.

Even in its most elementary form the Asiatic composite was a complex weapon which could only be invented by a people with a thorough understanding of the mechanics of bow action. Also, as Rausing (1967: 146) points out, it could not be developed until after the invention of pottery which permitted the boiling of glue. This raises the interesting question, originally posed by Pitt-Rivers, as to whether some form of the Eskimo bow similar to the plain D-bow (Type IV, Fig. 26) might not have been the prototype from which the true composites later evolved after glue became available. We shall return to this later.

In passing it should be mentioned that the Russian archaeologist Okladnikov has recovered antler "laths" used in composite bows from Neolithic graves near Lake Baikal (Chard, 1958: 10; Rausing, 1967: 119 and Fig. 60). The descriptions are contradictory, but the illustration of one of these "laths" indicates that they are similar to the strips of elk antler used by our Plains Indians in making the horn bow, a simplified form of the true composite which suddenly appeared upon the American high Plains along with the advent of the horse in the early 18th Century. I am not trying to imply that there can be any connection between the Baikal bows of around 2500 B.C. and the American horn bows of about 1700 A.D. other than similarity in design. However, some authority on horn bows should examine the Baikal specimens and determine definitely whether they were reflexed or not; for if they were, they could well represent some of the first examples of the true composite. As for the backing, sinew was probably used; it would appear pointless to back this form of antler belly with wood. It is certain the antler "lath" did not form the backing, as some anthropologists seem to think, for antler or horn simply cannot function under tension.

IG. 27.

FIG. 24.

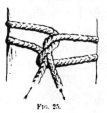

FIG. 25.

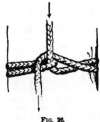

FIG. 26.

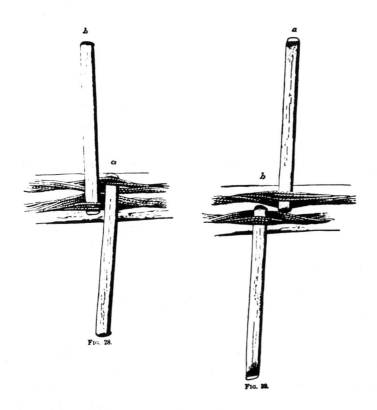

b

a

a

b

F₁ᴳ. 28.

Fıᴳ. 29.

FIGURE 27. Plate X from Murdoch's historic study of Eskimo bows showing how the sinew cords are added to the cable forming the back. Below at left are a peculiar clove hitch and to its right a reversed "soldier's hitch" used on an Eastern Siberian bow. Above are two views of an ivory tool which Murdoch proved was used to increase the tension of the cables making up the backs of the Eskimo bows. First are shown the positions of the tools at the completion of a half-turn; and second, their positions after they have been slipped through the twisted sinew cordage for beginning the next half-turn. "A Study of Eskimo Bows" by John Murdoch, SMITHSONIAN ANNUAL REPORT for 1884.

The feature which distinguishes the Asiatic composite from all others is the siyah or "ears." They are a rigid, non-flexible extension of the bow arm, set backward from the belly side at an even greater angle or curve than the reflex of the arm proper. This can be more easily understood by referring to the drawing of a Tartar bow which is shown both braced and relaxed (Fig. 28).

In some examples of the Asiatic composite, the combination of the reflexed arms and the siyahs gives the braced weapon the graceful Cupid's bow outline which is such a delight to the artist (Fig. 29). But the siyah was a practical refinement in design. To be effective, the siyah must have enough additional reflex when the bow is braced for the string between the knees to form an angle of approximately 20 degrees or more with the siyah itself (Fig. 25, "2"). In making the draw from "2" to "3" in the above figure, the effective length of the bowstring remains the distance between the bridges on the knees. However, as the depth of draw goes beyond the point "3", the angle between the siyah and the bowstring, which had reached zero at "3", gradually increases again until it reaches its maximum at "4". The siyah acts as a lever on the end of the bow arm, and its leverage increases as the angle increases from "3" to "4". This means that the bow arm itself can be designed to have a heavier weight, or pull, from points "3" to "4" than if there were no siyahs.

Translated into practical terms, this means that in comparing a well designed Asiatic composite with an equally well designed D-bow, both weighing 55 pounds at 28 inches of draw, the weight at 75 percent of full draw on the composite would be around 45 pounds while that of the straight bow would be only about 35 pounds. Upon release the two bows would each exert a thrust of 55 pounds upon the arrow during the first split-second, but the thrust of the bowstring on the composite would diminish at a much slower rate than on the straight bow. When back down to 75 percent of full draw the composite bowstring would be delivering 45 pounds of thrust, whereas the straight bow would have dropped down to 35 pounds. Furthermore, the instant the bowstring strikes the bridges at "3" it, in effect, shortens correspondingly, giving the arrow a still sharper snap as the string moves on down to bracing height (Fig. 25).

In summary, then, the siyah contributes in three ways to improved cast in the arrow: (1) It provides leverage for the bowstring so the bow can be designed to approach maximum weight earlier in the draw, allowing more energy to be stored for the cast. (2) Upon release, the bowstring imparts its energy to the arrow more uniformly and at a

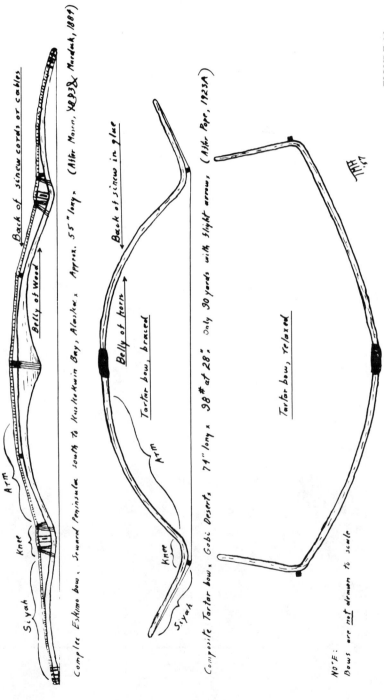

The Eskimo Tartar Type Bow & The Asiatic Prototype

Back of sinew cords or cables

Belly of Wood

Arm

Knee

Siyah

Complex Eskimo bow, Seward Peninsula south to Kuskokwim Bay, Alaska. Approx. 55" long. (After Mason, XEB3& Murdoch, 1884)

Back of sinew in glue

Belly of horn

Arm

Knee

Siyah

Tartar bow, braced

Composite Tartar bow, Gobi Desert. 74" long x 98# at 28". Only 90 yards with flight arrows. (After Pope, 1923A)

Tartar bow, relaxed

TRH
67

NOTE:
Bows are not drawn to scale

FIGURE 28.

79

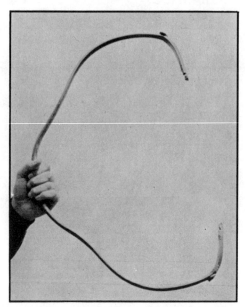

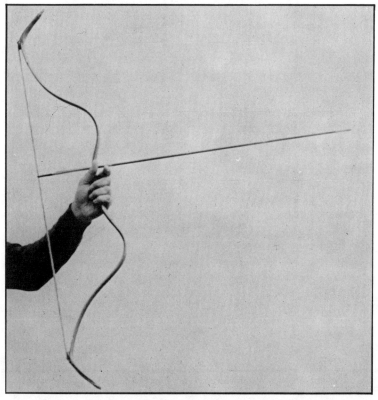

FIGURE 29. A light Korean composite shown relaxed, braced and at full draw. Note the rigid siyahs and the extreme flexing in the arms within a six to eight-inch span each side of the grip - a characteristic of the Asiatic composite. This feature is more pronounced in a target bow, such as this one, than in the larger and heavier weapons of this type. *Photo by Edward McEwen.*

higher and more sustained rate of thrust than in an ordinary bow without siyahs. And (3) when the bowstring reaches the bridges it is in effect shortened, increasing the tension again on the bowstring and giving the arrow a final snap as it leaves the bow.

The best study so far written on Eskimo bows appeared in the Annual Report of the U.S. National Museum for 1884, by John Murdoch. His interests were primarily centered on an attempt to differentiate between bows from the South, West and North of Alaska by the various ways the sinew cable backs were lashed to the wooden or antler bellies. Though he recognized that the "ears" indicated some sort of relationship to the Asiatic bows, and spoke of those having that feature as "Tartar-like," he naturally could not pursue this relationship further for lack of information then available. The draftsmanship illustrating his various classifications is so outstanding that included here are examples shown in four of his plates to point out the relationship of the Eskimo bow to the Asiatic composite.

In examining these drawings, four distinct variations are seen. The first, which I shall call Type I, has functional siyahs that abruptly turn back from the tips of the bow arms, as shown in Murdoch's Plate IV, Fig. 9 (Fig. 26). This particular bow, No. 89245, came from Point Barrow. The siyahs are mortised into the bow-limbs (Murdoch, 1884: 310). Unfortunately, no back or belly view of the bow is shown, but it looks like an uncompleted weapon to me. There are no bridges at the knees to prevent the bowstring from slipping past them when braced or shot, nor does it appear that the belly has been tillered enough to permit proper flexing in the arms. In spite of its shortcomings, this plate is used to illustrate that some Eskimo bows were built with siyahs which were intended to function. Balfour (1889: plate 5, Fig. 3) illustrates a similar bow with even more exaggerated siyahs.

In Type II, shown in Murdoch's Plate VII, Fig. 18, the siyahs are definitely vestigial, since they are not reflexed enough to function when the bow was braced: the bowstring would clear the knees before the draw began (Fig. 26). The tillering, as shown in both the side and back views, was such as would allow the siyahs to flex along with the rest of the arm. In making this bow it would have been just as well to do away with the artistic kinks in the ends of the arms and to complete it as a plain D-bow. This bow, No. 2505, was collected on the mainland of Siberia. It is a well made, efficient weapon, but not because of the siyahs, which contribute in no way to its efficiency.

A complex weapon whose action almost defies analysis is Type III, Murdoch's Plate VI, Fig. 5 (Fig. 26). This bow, No. 36028, came from near the mouth of the Kuskoquim River in Alaska, but the type was widely used. The bow of a Copper Eskimo (by G.H. Wilkins) shows one variation of this type at full draw (Fig. 30). Here almost all the flexing takes place between the grip and the knees, which is as it should be, but the siyahs, as in all Type III bows, are too long in proportion to the arms. This was done, apparently, to increase the depth of the draw; but the same could have been achieved, along with a better cast, if the extra wood had been put in the arms instead. These large, long, siyahs stuck on to the end of the arms only add to the total mass, and the inertia, upon release of the bowstring, causes an unnecessarily sluggish action.

Just how such an elaborate form evolved would be a study in itself. It was not only difficult to make, especially when the belly was composed of three separate pieces, as described by Jenness (1946: 122), but it was not so effective as Type II or the next form, Type IV, which will be described later. In the final analysis, Type III is a confusion in design between Type I and Type II, but I have felt justified in assigning it to a separate type because of its distinctive shape. Nelson (1899, Plate IX) shows four variations on this single theme.

As I have shown, the siyah in the Asiatic composite was not a foible, a fad or a stylish twist to the bow stave put there to delight the eye, but a very practical refinement in design which enabled some of the people of Asia to build bows that outshot all other bows, ancient or modern. On the other hand, it is hard to explain the presence of the siyah on the Eskimo bow other than as a vestigial remnant which has survived somehow through the ages since its original modification from the Asiatic composite. The Eskimo bow, with its brash wooden belly and free sinew back, simply does not lend itself to the refinement of the siyah.

Type IV, illustrated in Murdoch's Plate IV, Fig. 8, was an ordinary D-bow with a slight reflex when unbraced (Fig. 26). This was the best and most efficient of all Eskimo bow designs for, even when it was necessary to use two or three pieces of wood to make up the belly, the pressure exerted upon them by the sinew cables in the back, when the bow was brought to full draw, held them together as securely as though in a vise. With this bow, the Eskimo bowyer came of age: he had adopted all the worthwhile features of the Asiatic composite which applied to his time and place, and had discarded the rest as superfluous.

Incidentally, Saxton Pope (1923: 338) tested a Type IV bow. The belly was made of Douglas fir, 56 inches long. The weight was 80

FIGURE 30. A Copper Eskimo with a "Type III" bow at full draw. The influence of Asiatic composite design can be seen in the rigid siyahs, which have here become non-functional, and the amazing amount of flexing concentrated in the arms on either side of the grip. Compare with sketch of arrow release in Fig.37. This is the only front view of an Eskimo bow at full draw known to the author. *Photo by G.H. Wilkins, courtesy Geological Survey of Canada.*

pounds at 26 inches of draw and the cast was 180 yards. That was a weapon which would have been regarded with respect in England in the days of Edward III.

In the process of describing the Asiatic composite and the various forms of the Eskimo bow I believe I have shown it is self-evident that the latter was derived from the former. Just how, where or when this derivation took place cannot be answered until more certain knowledge has been obtained concerning the origin and evolution of the Asiatic composite, with particular emphasis upon the invention of the siyah and its spread to the North and Bering Strait.

It should be emphasized at this point that we are here concerned only with the Eskimo bow as we know it, and its relation to the Asiatic composite. It was not necessarily the first and only bow used in the Arctic. Nomadic groups following game and carrying self-bows, or even composites, could have made seasonal invasions penetrating possibly as far as the coastal regions of the Arctic Ocean; but a self or composite bow, even if it can be used under conditions of extreme cold — which is somewhat questionable — eventually is broken or lost and must be replaced. Under primitive conditions of trade a people living the year round in the Coronation Gulf or Cumberland Sound areas, for instance, must make bows from local materials which are capable of dependable service under all local climatic conditions.

Aside from the fact that the Eskimos made bows of driftwood and sinew — and antler or even bone when driftwood was not available — their genius lay in using a free sinew back in which the tension could be readily adjusted to meet varying conditions of humidity. Murdoch (1884: Plate XI) shows how this was done simply and quickly with two small ivory levers especially made for that purpose (Fig. 27). When we take the Eskimo way of life and environment into full consideration, we cannot conceive of a more successful solution of an almost impossible problem.

In returning to the question of the origin of the composite and the eventual evolution or modification of the Eskimo bow, there are two possible answers. As has been said, Pitt-Rivers, Balfour, Luschan and Adler all assumed that the composite was invented in some area where suitable bow-wood was not available, such as deserts where it was hot and dry. It may very well be found that the composite principle was conceived in some desert-like region, but it is questionable whether the scarcity of bow-wood sparked the first experiments with horn and sinew. After all, water buffalo, certainly the most popular if not the best provider of those two commodities in Asia, does not grow in deserts either! Of course, the horns and sinews of some desert animal could have been used in making up the first composites, but it must be remembered that not all horns have either the peculiar qualities or conformations which lend themselves to incorporation into the composite. Before accepting the hypothesis that necessity fostered the invention of the composite, a careful survey should be made of all horned animals on the entire Asiatic continent which lend themselves to the making of the composite, and the probabilities are that in one of those areas the composite came into being.

It may be found that in many of those regions suitable bow-wood also abounds, but I do not believe that would justify eliminating such areas from the list of candidates. The American horn bow certainly was not invented because of a lack of good bow-wood. Instead, I suggest that the American form of the composite represents a deliberate attempt to build a more efficient bow for use on horseback. This proposal is based upon the facts that (1) no archaeological evidence has been produced indicating that it existed before the introduction of the horse, and (2) that the materials, elk or mountain-sheep horn and deer sinew, are available in areas of North America where suitable bow-woods are easily come by.

All the evidence indicates that the American horn bow, a true composite, was based upon an already mature bowmaking tradition then utilizing suitable bow-woods, the reflex, and a thin sheet of sinew backing. The probabilities are that some American Indian bowmaker, who knew his trade thoroughly, conceived the idea of substituting horn for the belly half to take the compressive stresses, with a solid sinew back to stretch over it in the draw. All that remained was to solve the problems of cutting out the horn strips with the primitive tools at hand and making a glue which would hold the sinew back to the horn belly: no mean achievements in themselves. Early attempts to tiller the arms of horn and sinew to get proper flexing also caused considerable experimenting, but from the museum specimens still extant it is obvious that all these techniques eventually were worked out successfully.

Possibly, as with the American Indian, some Asian bowyer or bowyers brought about the invention of their composite during experiments in which a deliberate attempt was being made to produce a more efficient weapon than one which relied upon limbs of wood backed with a thin sheet of sinew — the reinforced bow.

That the scarcity of bow-wood fostered the invention of the composite is a possibility that must not be ruled out. However, if that suggestion is to be taken seriously, then Pitt-Rivers' other hypothesis should be reconsidered: that the concept of the composite originated in the North of Asia and then migrated to the South where it was perfected. In searching for the prototype, the Eskimo bows must be ruled out for reasons already mentioned, even though Murdoch (1884: 308 and Plate I, Fig. 1) felt that a D-bow from the Cumberland Sound area made of antler and sinew met the requirements. Though this bow and others like it do fit the theoretical concept of the composite prototype, they actually stand at the end of the line of Eskimo bow evolution; their crude appearance is a coincidence again dictated by the scarcity of materials.

Of course, it can be argued that the composite concept originated in the eastern part of Arctic North America, worked its way westward into Asia where it was perfected, and that then the siyah invaded the American Arctic, but that appears to be stretching the known facts a bit too far.

Instead, it is entirely possible that some of the plain Siberian bows with a free sinew back and no siyahs could be the modern representatives of the ancient prototype. Unfortunately, Adler's illustrator was not of Murdoch's caliber, nor are his descriptions as concise, so there is some question here. Also, the nomadic tendencies of the historic Asiatic peoples to drift with the herds would enable them to replenish their bow-wood annually and relieve, or even eliminate, the pressure to invent a bow with a free sinew back. This seems to me to be the weak point in the Northern origin hypothesis.

Assuming that in some way the use of a free sinew back did originate in the Arctic regions of Asia or North America, the next step in the evolution of the composite might be represented by the Lake Baikal bows discovered by Okladnikov. If it turns out that they were reflexed and had sinew backs, then they could represent some of the first utilizing glue and would give us an approximate date of 2000 to 3000 B.C. to mark that stage in the development.

The bows recovered from the Egyptian tombs — first reported by Luschan (1893), Longman (1894) and Balfour (1897) and recently discussed in detail by McLeod (1958 and 1962) — appear to be some of the first known examples utilizing the three components of horn, wood and sinew which are characteristics of the Asiatic composite as we know it today. These Egyptian weapons have the reflex; the only feature missing is the siyah. McLeod (1958: 398) dates them from about 1500 B.C. as did Luschan. Just where or when the siyah was first introduced is unknown, but there is a good possibility that it was a

Scythian innovation sometime around 400 B.C. However, that is little more than pure conjecture.

Here then are Pitt-Rivers' hypotheses modified by our present-day knowledge resulting from discoveries made during the years since he wrote. The Asiatic bows which Adler, Balfour and Luschan list from various museums in Germany, Russia and England should be sought out and reexamined. It is possible that a clearer picture of the birth and evolution of the Asiatic composite, as well as of the Eskimo bow, eventually will emerge.

6

The American Composite

The American composite, commonly called the horn bow, was mentioned briefly in the previous chapter. It is a weapon about which very little is known. It has been the subject of extravagant praise by men who saw it in use but had not enough curiosity to examine it, and today it is the most rare of all American bows: certainly not more than fifty of them are now extant. The descriptions of ten horn bows now in the U.S. National Museum will be found under Appendix B.

Basically, the design is simplicity itself. As mentioned in discussing the reinforced bows, when the sinew backing becomes too thick in relation to the wooden stave, the wood cells collapse and the bow-limb follows the string; it is impossible to maintain the reflex. By substituting a less compressible material, horn, for the wood in the belly of the bow-limb, this difficulty is overcome and the sinew backing can then increase until it represents approximately half the total thickness of the limb. In short, the sinew back*ing*, or lining, becomes a sinew *back*.

Since there is no limit, for all practical purposes, to the tensile stresses which can be imposed upon the sinew back, this permits the design of a short bow with a long draw. With this problem of a low bow-draw ratio solved, the reflex can then be increased far beyond that possible with the reinforced bow, and the net result is a short bow with high initial tension at bracing height and an excellent cast.

Whether the native American bowyers took full advantage of the possibilities inherent in the design of the horn bow can be questioned. As I have said, those who actually had an opportunity to witness its performance on the high Plains in the first half of the 19th Century failed to leave a satisfactory record. As will be seen, making the horn bellies for these bows is so forbidding a prospect that no investigator so far has had the courage to make replicas and, since it is impossible to take these old bows out and test them, about all that can be done at the moment is to piece stray bits of information together and try to estimate just how good they were.

Of course, the majority of these bows today are in rather sad condition, for most of them had seen hard use before they were collected, and lying around in superheated museum attic storerooms for a century or more has done them no good. However, there are two which seem to be particularly well preserved and might be considered type specimens of their respective varieties.

A short bighorn bow, catalogue No. 1/2707, in the American Museum of Natural History is probably as good an example of that particular type as any. Like most of those built upon ram's horn, this one is double-curved, and it can be argued that since it does not have a reflex it is not a composite; but it is perhaps best to overlook that detail for the moment. I have never handled this bow, but it appears in a photograph to be in perfect condition and of excellent workmanship (Fig. 4). In a letter dated 16 August 1956 Philip C. Gifford, Jr., lists the following dimensions: over-all length 37-3/4 inches; center of grip, 1 inch from belly to back by 1-1/2 inches wide; mid-limb, 19/32 by 1-1/2 inches; shoulder of nock, 9/16 by 21/32 inches.

At the Museum of the American Indian, Heye Foundation, there is a child's bow, catalogue No. 20/6557, 35 inches in length. When I saw it some years ago it was in perfect condition, but some well-meaning employee had carefully braced it by tying a string across its remarkably deep and uniform reflex. If in the meantime this bow has not been broken by someone tugging on the string, it is the most perfect specimen of an elkhorn bow which I have seen (Fig. 32).

It might be remarked, parenthetically, that it is really amazing how many reflexed bows I have seen braced backward through the years. The most certain way to destroy one's credibility at some museums is to attempt to explain the reflex. At one museum the curator actually walked off convinced that I was a fraud, leaving me standing in front of the case.

Of all those who visited the American West in the heyday of the horn bow only one, the artist Alfred Jacob Miller, examined it carefully and left us precise sketches of it in both the braced and relaxed positions (Fig. 31). His brief comments (Miller: 1951, 1968: 7) read:

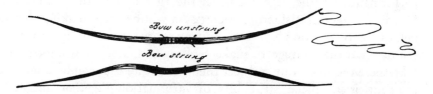

FIGURE 31.   Sketches of the elkhorn bow, unstrung and strung, by Alfred Jacob Miller. These are the only accurate portrayals left us by all those who saw it in use. *WEST OF ALFRED JACOB MILLER, edited by Marvin C. Ross; copyright 1951, 1968, by the University of Oklahoma Press.*

90

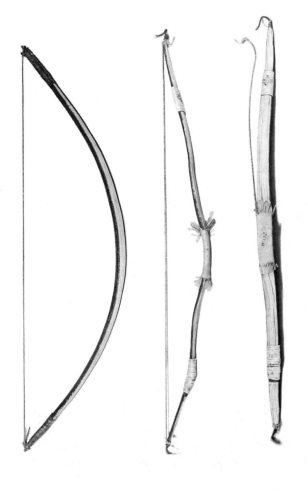

FIGURE 32. Two elkhorn bows, both shown braced backward. They are perfectly reflexed. The upper is the best example of the type seen in this study. It is 35 inches over all; 1 by ⅝ inches at the grip, ⅞ by ⅞ at mid-limb, and ⅜ by ⅜ below the nocks. The sinew back is slightly thicker than the elkhorn belly. Catalogue No. 20/6557. Collected among the Blackfoot. *Photo courtesy Museum of the American Indian, Heye Foundation.* The lower bow is shown in both side and belly views. It was made on the Fort Berthold Reservation around 1904–05, while the horn bow tradition was still remembered among the Hidatsa. *State Historical Society of North Dakota, courtesy Alan Woolworth.*

"The bow he carries in his hand is remarkable; it is made of Elk-horn with sinew strongly cemented on the outer-side . . .

"The bow unstrung is directly the reverse in form to that when strung; — a diagram will explain it."

Powell (1875:128), Wilson (1919:107), Clark (1884:78), Henry and Thompson (1897:713-4), Lowie (1924:246), Bradbury (1904:107), Kurz (1937:78 and 93) and others mention the bighorn bow, but superficially in each instance. Catlin (1857:32) so misunderstood the horn bow that he makes no mention of the sinew and argues that it was made from a bone taken from the jaw of the sperm whale and imported from the Pacific Coast by Indian traders. He reports that the Indians, when questioned about where the bow came from, said it was a "mystery," but it was Catlin who was gullible.

It is hard to imagine two more unpromising horns for the making of a composite than those from the mountain sheep ram and the elk, with their impossible twists and turns; but unfortunately for the Indian bowyer, there were no animals native to the Americas with large horns having a nice even sweep like those of the water buffalo or goat of Asia. Faris and Elmer (1945:161) in their excellent study, ARAB ARCH-ERY, observe that "a prime requisite of the horn for a bow should be that in its original state on the head it should have only a simple curvature in one plane." That the American bowmaker, with no other tools than a butcher knife and perhaps a hatchet, worked out a procedure whereby he could not only cut out the necessary strips of horn but straighten them — this accomplishment should receive recognition. When considered in the full context of the environment, the American composite stands with the Eskimo bow among the great triumphs of human ingenuity.

The flat statement that the horn bow appeared suddenly upon the American scene, and quite recently, invariably raises archaeological eyebrows. However, the lack of any sort of evidence indicating its existence before the early 1800's leads to the conclusion that 1700 A.D. is probably the very earliest date to which it can be assigned. If the American composite had been in use for the last five hundred years or so, fragments of the bow should be found in the refuse pits of open sites; for, unlike wooden bows, the horn belly lasts indefinitely. This is shown by the elk antlers excavated from the trash pits of the Missouri Indians, who lived in a much damper climate than that of the high Plains where the horn bows were primarily used.

George Metcalf, of the Smithsonian Institution, became interested in this question some years ago and searched through the material recovered from Indian sites on the Upper Missouri, where the horn bow was much in evidence during historic times. He found only two pieces, both of which were intermingled with gun caps, glass bottles and similar post-contact debris.

At the risk of repeating myself, my own theory is that the use of the horse in hunting and fighting forced the Plains Indians to modify their reinforced bow, and that the short sinew-lined Plains bow and the horn bow were developed at approximately the same time. If Catlin and others are to be believed, thousands of composites were to be seen in use on the high Plains and in the Great Basin during the first half of the 19th Century; but the reinforced bow was probably even more popular because it was far easier to make, and that possibly explains why there are more reinforced bows than composites in the museums.

Because of the limitations under which the Indian bowyer had to work, it is only natural to wonder how he managed to produce such a weapon. The best description yet published on the actual manufacture of horn bows, as far as I know, is that by Tiet (1927:97-8) in his study of the Coeur D'Alene. He states that a bow was made from a single piece of mountain ram's-horn, which had been split lengthwise and the "central piece taken out the full length." The horn was heated over a fire or boiled to make it pliable, and the outside of the horn formed the "inside of the bow." Apparently he means that the outside of the horn formed the face of the belly and the sinew back was glued to the inner side. The sinews used in the back were taken from the legs of deer, cut off as long as possible and dried. "When to be used they were thoroughly crushed with stone hammers and mauls until they were quite pliable and torn into shreds. They were then glued the entire length of the back of the bow with a glue made of salmon skins. After the first layer of sinew was glued on, the bow was wound with pa'telen bark and hung up to dry and set. In a few hours it was taken down and a new layer glued on." The final back was from 5 to 10 millimeters thick (.2 to .4 of an inch), and from 20 to 30 leg sinews were needed to make a good bow.

A peculiar statement of Tiet's is that as each layer of sinew was put on it was cut practically through with a knife every 5 centimeters or so "at right angles to the length of the bow stave." That simply does not make sense, for it would be self-defeating to cut the sinew-back into short pieces. Also Tiet makes no mention of soaking the sinew in the glue before applying it.

A much more detailed account of the process is in the unpublished field notes of Gilbert L. Wilson covering the material culture of the Hidatsa. This information was recorded by him in 1910 "based upon a narrative by Wolf-chief in which he recalled the method followed by his father, Small-ankles. Wolf-chief was fifteen years old when he watched his father make the bow while they were encamped on the Little Missouri early in the fall. The bow was constructed over a period of two weeks."

The elkhorns were picked up after being shed, the tines chopped off with a butcher knife and "the concave side of each arm of the bow" — probably the inner side of the horn — was worked down to about the final thickness.

When the two parts for the bow-limbs reached this stage, a small trench about one foot deep was dug, the parts of elk antler were put into the trench, then covered with dirt, and water was poured on the dirt. This addition of dirt and water was repeated three times until the trench was half filled, after which it was filled with dry earth on which a fire was built. When the fire had burned about twenty-four hours the steam in the mud had softened the antlers until they could be bent into the final shape for the bow, which they then retained. If they were not sufficiently pliable when first tried, a longer steaming was required.

After cooling came the final trimming to thickness and width. Then the antlers were again moistened and heated over the fire. If found pliable they were given their final shape and held in position with large rocks until they had cooled and set. Only the concave side was shaved down, while the other was merely smoothed and polished.

The two bow-limbs were spliced together with a long sloping cut. The flat surfaces of this splice, where the glue was applied, were roughened and four holes were drilled through the splice. Glue was then applied to the two opposing surfaces of the splice, the two arms were joined, and soaked deer tendons were passed through the four holes and drawn tight. As the wet tendons dried they pulled the glued surfaces together. Once the glue in the splice had dried, the tendons were trimmed off flush with the surface of the grip.

The notches for the bowstring were then cut: two opposing each other in the upper limb tip and only one notch on the left edge of the lower limb tip.

The sinew for the back was then shredded and the threads laid out longitudinally. The back of the horn belly was scored to hold the glue, and the glue was applied to about eight inches beginning at the nock. Some shredded sinew was then fastened at the nock with a temporary

94

whipping and pressed down into the glue. As a result about eight inches of sinew extended over onto the unglued section of the back. More glue was then applied over the sinew and allowed to soak in. The next section of the back received an application of glue, the second bunch of sinew worked down into the glue, and so on until the entire back had been covered with a continuous layer of glue and sinew from nock to nock.

The sinew and glue back was given a final polishing with a buffalo rib and the sinew at the nocks was given a permanent binding with sinew threads.

According to Wolf-chief, only one application of sinew and glue was put on the elkhorn bow. At no place does he indicate the relative thickness of horn and sinew. Nor does he state specifically which side of the worked antler faced the sinew back.

The bowstring was tied permanently at the upper nock and a noose was used to hold the string in the lower single notch.

In freezing weather the elk-horn bow was extremely cold, so the grip had to be bound with buckskin to protect the bow hand.

In making the bow from mountain sheep horn, the horns were chopped off close to the skull with an axe. A shallow trench was dug following the outline of the horn and a horn was placed in the trench. A small fire was then built against or near the root of the horn until it was scorched. Apparently, the only way the horn could be worked was by scorching and cutting the burnt parts. It took approximately half a day to cut away the concave side of one horn and remove the pith.

Hot stones, twice the size of the fist, were used to soften the horn for cutting in the final stages of shaping. Eventually, the horn was reduced to a thin strip about three fingers wide.

The two horn strips were given their final shape by rubbing them with mountain sheep fat, and heating them again with stones. Three pegs were driven into the ground to hold them in the desired curve while they set.

Apparently the splice in the grip was made in much the same way as in the elkhorn bow, except that in this instance four square-headed iron nails were used after first drilling the necessary holes.

Wolf-chief does not elaborate on how the sinew back was applied to the horn. Presumably the same procedure was followed as with the elkhorn bow.[1]

[1] The information of Wolf-chief's narrative is taken from a transcript of Dr. Gilbert L. Wilson's field notes made available through the courtesy of the American Museum of Natural History.

In spite of the many questions left unanswered, Wolf-chief's account is by far the best we have of how the American composite was made. It is unfortunate that he did not go into greater detail, for example on the amount of sinew constituting the back, or whether the bow was being reflexed or double-curved when the limbs were shaped; but it is understandable that he might overlook or forget some details when he was trying to remember a procedure observed in his boyhood.

Incidentally, Wilson further reports that a Mandan named Willie Hale, living in 1912 on the Fort Berthold Reservation, told him that his father also had made elkhorn bows. According to him, the two pieces of antler were boiled at one end and the other in a large kettle. At the end of five days [!] the horn limbs were easily bent into shape by inserting them between the projecting logs at the corner of the cabin.

Wolf-chief's comments about the relative merits of the two kinds of horn bow are puzzling, for he says that the elkhorn was actually not much of a weapon; that it was pretty and valued chiefly by the young men as something showy with which to strut around the village. On the other hand, he says that the bow made from ram's horn was a good bow. The latter, with ten arrows, was worth a good horse when horses were scarce. It was used in both hunting and war and had a better cast than a wooden bow; it was difficult to become accustomed to a wooden bow after having used one of ram's horn.

This statement was a genuine surprise to me, for it had been my impression that most, if not all, bighorn bows were originally double-curved and not reflexed, as are all of the elkhorn. Furthermore, on the whole — there are exceptions — the workmanship of the elkhorn is superior to that of the bighorn.

The question whether one or the other actually was superior probably will never be decided, since these old bows cannot be endangered by shooting them, and, though there is no doubt replicas of the elkhorn bow will eventually be made, since their antlers can be picked up after shedding, it would require the sacrifice of a trophy head today to make one of mountain sheep horn. But, as far as the effectiveness of the elkhorn bow itself is concerned, with all due respect to the Indians' love for display, it hardly seems reasonable that they would go to all that work to build an inferior weapon. The least we can do is credit the Indian bowmakers with common sense, and work from the premise that they invested their time and labor in straightening out the elkhorn for the practical reason that it would produce a bow superior in performance to the reinforced.

The documentary evidence on the performance of the elkhorn is almost as scarce as the descriptions; the sole exception again being Alfred Jacob Miller (1951 and 1968). Miller was fascinated with Indian archery, for he makes repeated references to it in his notes.

"Now if an Elk-horn was carried to the smartest Yankee we have, with a request to make a bow of it, the probability is, that, for once, he would not find it convenient to attempt it [p. 7].

"While Indians are resting in camp, one of their amusements . . . is a trial of skill with the Elk-horn bow . . .

"With an Elk-horn bow, they sometimes drive an arrow completely through a Buffalo, its propelling power being greater than that of a Yew bow. In the Buffalo chase it is most effective, striking the animal in almost any part is fatal — his every movement causing the arrow to vibrate — thus cutting him to pieces [p. 60].

". . . and from the Elk-horns they make their most efficient bows [p. 140].

"The Elk are desirable game to the Indians on account of their size and weight . . . They secure the skins . . . used for leggins, and of their horns, measuring sometimes over five feet, they construct their best bows" [p. 158].

Other journalists mention the bighorn bow. Bradbury (1904:107) observes that on the upper Missouri in 1810 the price of a bow made of Osage orange was a horse and a blanket and that one of these was "little inferior" to a bighorn bow, which implies that the bois d'arc bow was very good indeed. Henry and Thompson (1897:713-4), in speaking of the bighorn bow, say, "These neat bows are about three feet long, and throw an arrow an amazing distance . . . I have known a Piegan to give a gun and a horse for one of this made of sinew."

Belden (1875:111) declares he saw a bighorn bow shoot 500 yards. In spite of the fact that Belden appears to be exactly what he says — a man who had lived among the Sioux for some years and apparently had every reason to know what he was talking about — such a claim in cast for any American composite strikes me as ridiculous. It is doubtful whether even an Asiatic composite could have cast a Plains arrow 500 yards under the most favorable conditions, for it must be remembered that all flight records are shot with arrows having very small fletching and especially designed for achieving maximum distance. At about the same time that Belden was writing, the English champion, Ford, was establishing his best record of 307 yards 1 foot (Longman and Walrond, 1894:428), which compares favorably with the Old English flight shots mentioned by Shakespeare.

Shallow: [Old Double] dead! a' drew a good bow; and dead! a' shot a fine shoot; John of Gaunt loved him well, and betted much money on his head. Dead! a' would have clapped i' the clout at twelve score; and carried you a forehand shaft a fourteen and a fourteen and a half, that it would have done a man's heart good to see. (KING HENRY IV, PART TWO, Act III, Scene II)

It is generally agreed that a "forehand shaft" corresponds to what we would call a flight arrow today, indicating that among the old English archers 280 to 290 yards was considered remarkable shooting under favorable conditions.

In an attempt to find out more about the American composites, I again turned to Mr. Koeppen and Mr. Bendtsen of the National Wood Products Laboratory at Madison, Wisconsin. A ram's horn not being available, two pieces of elkhorn were sent them for testing. Because of the physical peculiarities of elkhorn, both its natural twisting and the pith in its center, the pieces failed in compression at 13,000 and 15,000 pounds per square inch respectively, but the report read as follows:

"Buckling occurred due to the curvature in the specimens, decreasing the load required for failure. Also, the porous material in the center portions of the horns probably contributes little to strength. If this material was removed before testing . . . maximum crushing strengths would probably be doubled." (Bendtsen, 1966)

In other words, the crushing strength of the outer portion of the elkhorn, which was actually used in making the bow, is probably in the neighborhood of 26,000 to 30,000 pounds per square inch. When these crushing strengths are compared with those of the various bow-woods given in the chapter on the reinforced bow, it seems that we are definitely on the trail of a superior bow design.

A watercolor by Alfred Jacob Miller (1951 and 1968:189) entitled "Indians Testing Their Bows" possibly holds the answer to the question: Did the horn bow achieve the full possibilities inherent in its design? The draw shown in the painting is a full 30 inches if the Indian is using the Tertiary release, and that length is further substantiated by the length of the arrows shown sticking in the ground beside the arrowmaker at the left in the picture (Fig. 36). They certainly are not the 22 to 24 inch arrows normally associated with Plains bows. Furthermore, the degree of flexing shown — the bow-draw ratio — could not possibly be achieved with anything other than a horn bow. In fact, the curvature of the bow being shot agrees perfectly with the theoretical ideal.

If this were a photograph, it would be justifiable to say that the question was definitely settled in the affirmative, but there always remains the doubt that Miller accurately portrayed here the true

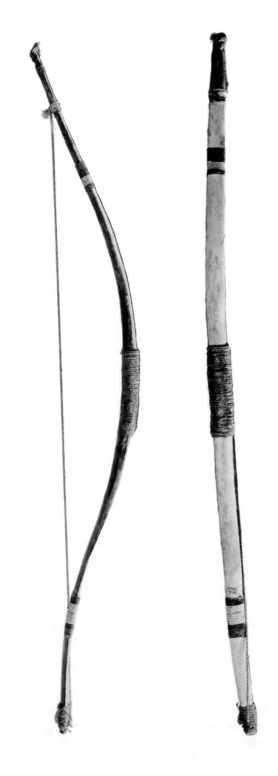

FIGURE 33. An elkhorn bow strung correctly, as shown by the knot at the left nock. It is relaxed with the noose caught on the sinew seizing above the lower nock, as seen at the right. The bow is 43¼ inches long over all; 1³⁄₁₆ by 1¹⁵⁄₃₂ inches wide at the grip, 2¹⁄₃₂ by 1³⁄₁₆ at mid-limb, and ¹⁷⁄₃₂ by 1³⁄₁₆ wide immediately below the nocks. Collected among the Hidatsa by the Rev. Gilbert L. Wilson in 1912. Catalogue No. 50. 1/7363. *The American Museum of National History.*

proportions of bow length to length of draw. From his various comments previously quoted, it is obvious that he was fascinated with the horn bow and how expertly the Shoshone handled it. His sketch of the bow in its relaxed and braced positions proves that he was far more accurate and intelligent in his observations of the horn bow than any of his contemporaries (Fig. 31). Therefore, it seems reasonable to assume that the proportions of bow length to length of draw are accurate, and that we can safely conclude that some makers of the horn bow, at least, did produce weapons capable of making the casts which were theoretically possible in its basic design.

A further confirmation of this conclusion is still another of Miller's watercolors bearing almost the same title, "Snake Indians – Testing Bows" (Miller, 1951 and 1968:60). This depicts two archers: one just after release and the second with the arrow at about two-thirds of full draw, or about 26 inches (Fig. 34). The arrow itself will allow a 30-inch draw. If my estimate of 26 inches is correct, then the bow scales very close to 52 inches between the nocks, or it is, as shown, at a 2 to 1 bow-draw ratio, with an indicated ratio of 1.74 to 1 at 30 inches!

A possible variation of the American composite could be the elusive buffalo rib bow. Even less information on this weapon has been found than on those of elkhorn or bighorn. Although I had noted a few scattered and fleeting references to the buffalo rib bow from time to time I had never taken its existence seriously until it was mentioned in a letter from Judge F.B. Zahn of Fort Yates, North Dakota, dated 19 August 1956.

Judge Zahn was the son of William Zahn, a soldier who had been stationed at Fort Abraham Lincoln at the time of the battle of the Little Big Horn, and who was on the burial detail after the Custer fight. After his discharge in 1876, William Zahn married a Sioux girl and remained among the Sioux as a trader. He died on 3 September 1936 after living among the Plains Indians for sixty-seven years. F.B. Zahn also spent his life among the Sioux and considered himself one of them, constantly working for their betterment.

In response to a letter of mine asking for more information on the buffalo rib bow, Judge Zahn wrote in a letter dated 18 September 1956:

"From what I could gather here and there from oldtime Indians the buffalo rib bows were excellent. For one thing they lasted longer than wooden bows. Just yesterday I talked to Spotted Bear (age 96 years) and he said as a young man he saw quite a few rib bows. This type of bow was also used to count COUP on an

FIGURE 34. "Snake Indians — Testing Bows." A watercolor by Alfred Jacob Miller of the elkhorn bow in action. *WEST OF ALFRED JACOB MILLER, by Alfred Jacob Miller, edited by Marvin C. Ross; copyright 1951, 1968, by the University of Oklahoma Press.*

enemy as well as to strike him a heavy blow. A wooden bow would break. Spotted Bear recalls the horn bows. He said the western enemy Tribes used them."

From a letter dated 4 January 1957;

"[The Indians'] canvas covered the sinew [backing on their bows] so that rain or moisture would not soften the sinew and thus loosen the bows' splicing."

Judge Zahn describes the making of buffalo rib bows as follows:

"Buffalo ribs are much smaller than those of the horse or cow; they are also thinner and much more flexible — hence made very desirable bow material. The Sioux used sandstone to thin the ribs where they were to be spliced. Before the splices were joined, two notches or grooves were made and then wet sinew was wrapped around them; then a coating of glue made from a gelatinous substance formed by boiling buffalo hooves was applied over the sinew [and] the grooved section was again wrapped completely with wet sinew. When dry, the spliced section was held together firmly. The slenderizing of bow-ends and notches were formed by using sandstone. Sandstone was the Indian's file."

In 1958 I interviewed Spotted Bear, reputed at that time to be 98, in Judge Zahn's company. Spotted Bear was blind, but when the Judge placed a bow in his hands, and I saw how he held it and nocked the arrow, there remained no question in my mind that he had had a long and intimate acquaintance with that weapon. Spotted Bear assured me, through Judge Zahn as our interpreter, that the Sioux had made many bows from the ribs of buffalo. From his description, it was clear that the bow had a heavy back of sinew, a question which Judge Zahn had left unanswered in his letter. I could not satisfy myself as to whether it had a reflex or not, primarily because of the difficulty of conveying the question to a man who could not see the sketch I made for the Judge. Spotted Bear did say that the Sioux originally "thought out the bow for themselves," and that, "before the horse came, the bow was longer and shot farther." Those two statements, whether right or wrong, indicated a sense of history I never expected to encounter in that old warrior.

As has been said, there are probably not fifty American composites extant. During all the years I have worked on this problem, only twenty-four have been located and of these I have actually seen and handled only seventeen. Because of their rarity, as well as their age and present condition, these bows cannot be drawn nor shot and any conclusions must be based upon theory rather than practical experience. If or when replicas can be made and shot, these theoretical conclusions may undergo radical revision.

At this point the hypothesis about the function of the horn belly in the American composite may be stated as follows: when the thickness of the sinew-back becomes too great in relation to that of the belly when made of wood, the wood cells collapse and the bow-limb follows the string. Therefore, in order to withstand these greater compressive stresses and maintain the reflex, the belly must be made of horn.

In trying to determine in retrospect just how these conclusions took form, I believe that the reinforced Plains bow has probably had more influence upon my thinking than the horn; primarily because there are more of them and because I have several in my own collection for reference. Also, my experience in working with Asiatic composites in the Turkish and Korean forms has undoubtedly had its influence.

Insofar as the reinforced bows are concerned, I have seen nothing to challenge my conclusions that there is a very definite and delicate balance between the thickness of the sinew backing, or lining, and that of the wooden bow-limb which must withstand the compressive stresses. Where there has been deformation of the bow-limb in the reinforced bow, the sinew backing is usually heavier than normally found. Because the vast majority of reinforced bows still maintain enough of their reflex to show that they were not double-curved originally, I conclude that those which appear to have been made up as double-curved bows have become that way through use rather than intent; they were put into service before the wood was thoroughly seasoned, the sinew backing was too heavy, or they were left braced too long after being collected. The possibility is not to be overlooked that some of them may actually have been made up double-curved, but I believe they represent a very small minority. In short, I have observed nothing, so far as the reinforced bows are concerned, which would challenge this hypothesis about the function of the horn belly in the American composite.

Strangely enough, the entire concept of the function of the horn belly is thrown into doubt by one bow, built strictly along the lines of the better specimens of the elkhorn bow. This bow is without question the most spectacular example of the American composite yet found (Fig. 35). It is expertly made and, though one often reads that the horn bows were covered with snakeskin to protect the sinew-back from moisture, this is the only one I have seen which was so protected. But it has a wooden belly!

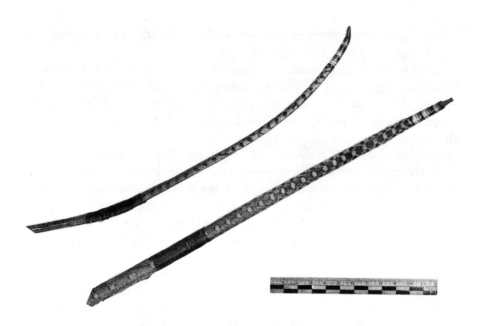

FIGURE 35.   An American composite attributed to the Flatheads. The only snakeskin-covered bow yet seen by the author. A wooden lath was used instead of an elkhorn belly, indicating the maker never intended that the bow be shot. In all probability it was made up to be pawned off on an unsuspecting white man, since no Indian would buy a bow without having tested it. *U.S. National Museum. Catalogue No. 9043.*

This bow, catalogue No. 9043, I discovered in the U.S. National Museum about thirteen years ago when R.A. Elder, Jr., and George Metcalf, both of the Smithsonian Institution, were showing me through the bow collections in the National Museum. I have never forgotten its existence nor misplaced my notes describing it, but as the evidence in favor of the horn belly mounted I began to doubt the accuracy of my identification of the material in the belly as wood and concluded that I had been mistaken. Finally, toward the close of this study, I wrote the Smithsonian asking that the bow be withdrawn from storage and re-examined. In a letter on 27 March 1970, Mr. Metcalf replied that the belly was indeed made of wood and that it appeared to be of red cedar.

That settles that question, but it raises many others: the chief one being how could a bow, built along classic elkhorn lines but with a wooden belly, maintain its reflex? This should be as impossible as a scientifically established instance of levitation.

As I remember this bow, its reflex was flawless. The snakeskin cover on one limb was badly tattered, which explains why only the one limb and the grip were photographed — something I have regretted ever since. Possibly, because of its elegance, I could fall back on the standard explanation of the inexplicable by calling it a "ceremonial" bow, but the dirt and grime with which a sweaty bow-hand apparently has stained the grip seem proof enough that it has seen hard service.

This bow, a little over 43-1/2 inches long, is attributed to the Flatheads. In a letter dated 7 May 1970, Mr. Metcalf says it was collected by Dr. James T. Ghiselein of the U.S. Army while stationed at Fort Colville, Washington Territory, sometime during 1868. When I saw it it had a perfect reflex, measuring six inches from the belly side of the grip to a line running from one nock to the other, and seven inches when measured to the ends of the tips. In a previous letter, dated 14 April 1970, Metcalf had reported the following dimensions in centimeters taken at 10-centimeter intervals, or stations, beginning immediately below the shoulders of one of the nocks:

Station	Width	Total thickness	Thickness of wooden belly
0 cm.	1.4 cm.	1.1 cm.	?
10 cm.	1.9 cm.	1.3 cm.	.5 cm.
20 cm.	2.2 cm.	1.4 cm.	.5 cm.
30 cm.	2.45 cm.	1.4 cm.	?
40 cm.	2.6 cm.	1.45 cm.	.5 cm.
50 cm.(approx. center)	2.85 cm.	2.0 cm.	?
60 cm.	2.6 cm.	1.65 cm.	.6 cm.
70 cm.	2.4 cm.	1.45 cm.	?
80 cm.	2.2 cm.	1.4 cm.	.45 cm.
90 cm.	2.0 cm.	1.25 cm.	.6 cm.
100 cm.	1.7 cm.	1.35 cm.	?
103.6 cm.(other nock)	1.5 cm.	1.25 cm.	.5 cm.

Where question marks are shown, Metcalf was unable to measure the thickness of the wooden belly because of the snakeskin cover.

The ratio of the sinew-back to the horn belly in the American composite is usually one to one; each representing approximately one-half the total thickness of the bow-limb. In this Flathead bow, the wooden belly represents more nearly one-third than one-half of the total limb thickness. This in itself should indicate it was not a practical working bow. In spite of what appear to be sweat stains on its grip, I doubt whether bow No. 9043 was ever braced, much less shot.

The probabilities are that it was made up by some expert bowyer with the idea of selling it to one of the officers stationed at Fort Colville. Since he knew that the bow would not be shot by its white owner, he substituted a cheap lath of wood in place of the elkhorn belly and tastefully covered his deception with the skin of two snakes, head to head at the grip. A moist grimy hand applied a few times to the grip gave the bow the used look necessary further to insure its sale.

FIGURE 36. "Indians Testing Their Bows" — A Miller watercolor of Shoshones displaying their skill with the elkhorn bow. *WEST OF ALFRED JACOB MILLER,* edited by Marvin C. Ross; copyright 1951, 1968, by the University of Oklahoma Press.

7

The Plains Bow In Action

Any attempt to present an objective evaluation of the natives of North America as archers must, of necessity, be limited to the Plains Indians. This is because they are nearer to us in time and were more closely observed by more individuals keeping journals or writing military reports than was the case during the early days of exploration and colonization in the East. Also, where accounts of Indian marksmanship do appear in the documents of the 16th to 18th Centuries, they tend to reflect more the general gullibility of the age than the serious pursuit of facts.

Perhaps the most repeated wondertale is the one which Hansard (1841:25) — who welcomed everything of this sort as grist for his mill — credited to Alexander Cockburn who

"says he has seen them stand perhaps a hundred yards from a bird feeding upon the ground, and, by shooting directly upwards, cause the arrow to pin it to the earth; and mentions as a further instance of their skill, that they would stick a shaft upright, and, retiring a great way off, shoot perpendicularly as before, when the arrow so shot descended upon the other which was fixed in the ground, and split it in two."

And Hansard apparently was an experienced archer.

Judge Zahn, whose description of the buffalo rib bow was quoted in the previous chapter, is a little more factual. From a letter dated 19 August 1956:

"Your inquiry concerning the Sioux Indian archery brought back many memories of my boyhood, as I was born in a teepee and reared among the Plains Indians, particularly the Hunkpapa (Sitting Bull's Band) and the Yanktonai division of the Dakota Sioux. What I am about to relate to you, therefore, is what I have actually seen and not what I have read in books.

"I still vividly recall an Indian (Sioux) named Swift Hawk who used to make us bows and arrows. With these weapons, the bows of which were about 25 to 30 inches in length we hunted cotton-tails, skunks, and other small game. We used to kill them at close range.

"Sioux bows were made of ash or hickory. The length of these bows varied in length from 45 to 48 inches. Bow strings were made from heavy sinew rolled when wet. No other material was ever used. Bows were made from buffalo ribs by splicing them in the middle and wrapping or taping them with heavy sinew. The wristguard was made from parfleche or rawhide. As a decoration some Indians encased their bows with the skin of a bull-snake. Arrows were from choke-cherry and June-berry stems. The length of Sioux arrows was anywhere between 18 to 24 inches long. I have seen bows that were not sinew backed. I have seen arrows that did not have iron points, but were sharp and pointed though some had blunt points. In order to harden the point the arrow-maker held them over a low fire. I once knew an Indian, Brave Buffalo (Medicine-man) who had a quiver of arrows with parfleche points. He said he used them to stun small game, and then he would kill them at close range. The short serviceable bows were about 38 inches long. The double curved bows were easy to insert and withdraw from the parfleche case. I have in my possession a parfleche quiver with a 'D' bow about 48 inches long. In war, when a warrior did not have a COUP stick, he used his bow in counting coup.

"About the year 1898, I saw Sharp-horn-bull, a Yanktonai Sioux, kill a wild Texas longhorn steer with a bow and arrow during a mid-summer festival for exhibition. He used only one arrow and rode bareback with a parfleche thong, which served as a bridle, tied on the lower jaw of his buffalo pony. The steer was chased out of a corral at full speed and Sharp-horn-bull, quirting his pony, rode up to the animal [right side] as he affixed the arrow to the bow-string with the bow held arms length above him. He pulled the arrow back and brought the bow swiftly down, releasing his grasp on the arrow. The steer dropped fast."

From a letter dated 18 September 1956:

"The bow was unstrung [when not in use]; however, the sinew bow-string attached to the double-notched end remained permanently, while the single notch at the opposite end was utilized for un-stringing the bow. All sinew or rawhide was soaked in water before using it for bowstrings, ropes, thongs, encasing warclub handle, and all other purposes. Knots were not employed in fastening the sinew to the bow, but while wet, was twisted below a top loop and never tied.

"The Sioux [were not] acquainted with Osage-orange bow-wood to my knowledge.

"What was the Sioux estimate of the bow as a weapon? It was their main weapon and served its purpose excellently; better than the muzzle-loader; better than the cap and ball revolver. The Sioux say that the gun takes too long to load to make it an estimable weapon — also too noisy.

"[In the Custer fight] the Sioux used war-clubs, bows and arrows, and lances in closest combat — there were very few guns. Approximately 65 of the various Sioux Bands — Hunkpapa, Sans Arch, Ogalala, Minneconoju [were killed]; I do not know the number of Cheyennes who were killed. Approximately 264 [white] officers and enlisted men [were killed].

"How many arrows did the Sioux carry when hunting or on the warpath? About 20 arrows. During a buffalo hunt, the Sioux kept one arrow in his mouth and one on the bow-string. Sioux experts in the use of the bow and arrow were: Stone, Holy Horse, Brave Buffalo, Iron Bull, Sharp-horn-bull — to name only an outstanding few. Four Horns, Black-foot Tribe, Montana, killed seven mature buffalos with seven arrows; some of the arrows went entirely through the buffalos — a feat very difficult to beat!"

From notes of my interview with Spotted Bear, I see that he also said Sharp-horn-bull was a famous archer, who, with four arrows in his mouth and one in the bow, could shoot the five before the first hit the ground. Spotted Bear also said the Sioux's usual target was a moccasin hung on a stick which had been stuck in the ground. The Judge explained that they shot at it standing from a distance of approximately 45 yards. One of Sharp-horn-bull's favorite tricks was to shoot at a moccasin thrown in the air as he rode past at full gallop. He did not always hit.

Sharp-horn-bull's feat at the "game of the arrow," as Catlin (1857:141-2) calls it, is quite believable since, in Catlin's version, an expert could get eight arrows into the air before the first hit the ground; a possible exaggeration of an arrow or two.

Dr. James H. Howard, the anthropologist, once described to me another variation of the moccasin shoot which he had observed among the Teton Dakota at Little Eagle, South Dakota, on 4 July 1947. The actual target was a spot the size of a quarter marked with charcoal on the sole of a moccasin. Native bows with steel-tipped arrows were used. The contestants took turns riding past the target at full gallop, releasing their arrows at a distance of about five feet. The third man up hit the target dead center and won a prize of one dollar.

Tixier (1940:253-4), who went on an extended hunt with the Osage in the early 1800's, describes a shooting-match. The target was a piece of meat about 6 inches square placed 20 paces behind a barrier of brush. Each man took his shot at full gallop and the majority of 200 arrows were in a cluster 2 feet in circumference.

The fact that various individuals assign a length of 3 feet or less to these bows intrigues me, for I have yet to see a self or reinforced bow of that length in our museums which was anything other than a boy's bow. If, the estimates are correct, and not minimized for effect, then these must have been composites — and I am unaware of composites among the Osage. George Catlin (1857:142) also speaks of these short bows in what appears to be an objective description of the Plains Indians' skill in handling the weapon:

"For the successful use of the bow, as it is used through all this region of country on horseback, and invariably at full speed, the great object of practice is to enable the bowman to draw the bow with suddenness and instant effect; and also to repeat the shots in the most rapid manner. As their game is killed from their horses' backs while at the swiftest rate — and their enemies fought in the same way; and as the horse is the swiftest animal of the prairie, and always able to bring his rider alongside, within a few paces of his victim; it will easily be seen that the Indian has little use in throwing his arrow more than a few paces; when he leans quite low on his horse's side, and drives it with astonishing force, capable of producing instant death to the buffalo, or any other animal in the country . . . The effects produced by [these bows] at the distance of a few paces is almost beyond belief, considering their length, which is not often over three, — and sometimes not exceeding two and a half feet. It can easily be seen, from what has been said, that the Indian has little use or object in throwing the arrow to any great distance. And as it is very seldom that they can be seen shooting at a target, I doubt very much whether their skill in such practice would compare with that attained to in many parts of the civilized world; but with the same weapon, and dashing forward at fullest speed on the wild horse, without the use of the rein, when the shot is required to be made with the most instantaneous effect, I scarcely think it possible that any people can be found more skilled, and capable of producing more deadly effects with the bow."

The Judge's description of Sharp-horn-bull's draw and release — the arrow being drawn as the bow is brought to bear and released as it comes on target — seems to be characteristic of the Plains Indian shooting. Spotted Bear demonstrated it to me, as did Remington Schuyler, the artist who was a trader on the Rosebud Reservation when a young man. Schuyler said that speed and accuracy at relatively short distances described it best. The targets chosen were always small — a tuft of grass, a clod of dirt or a chunk of wood. The draw, aim and release were all in one motion.

At this point it might be well to dispel some misconceptions about the Tertiary release of Morse (Fig. 37). In spite of all the nonsense written about the superiority of the Mediterranean or the Mongolian over the Tertiary, the truth of the matter is that they are all equally powerful. With a little experimenting anyone can quickly settle that question for himself. Of course, one must practice the Tertiary long enough to get the feel of it, but it can draw any weight bow just as satisfactorily as the other two. With the short Plains bows it has the added advantage of not pinching the nail of the index finger against the nock, at full draw, which I find very annoying. My main criticism of the Tertiary is that my unprotected fingers quickly become sore, so I am thinking of departing from tradition far enough to experiment with a

110

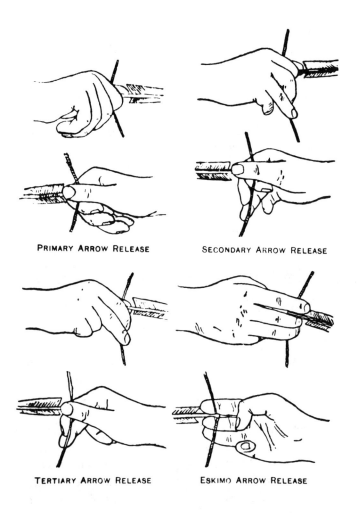

PRIMARY ARROW RELEASE   SECONDARY ARROW RELEASE

TERTIARY ARROW RELEASE   ESKIMO ARROW RELEASE

FIGURE 37. The various arrow releases as originally described by Morse (1885). The Mongolian, in which the bowstring is engaged by the thumb alone, is not shown since it was used primarily in Asia. The Mediterranean release is the same as the Eskimo. *BULLETIN 30, Bureau of American Ethnology.*

glove of some sort. An ordinary light leather work glove, with the index and thumb cut off, should not be too awkward after some practice.

Alfred Jacob Miller, the previously mentioned artist who drew the sketch of the elkhorn bow (Fig. 31), observes in one of his notes (1951, 1968:60):

> "While [Snake] Indians are resting in camp one of their amusements is a trial of skill with the Elk-horn bow . . .
>
> "They are careful to select a calm day and at a distance of 30 or 40 yards, strike within the circumference of a quarter of a dollar. The arrow is tipped with iron, and feathering remarkable for its neatness, giving a poise true and equal, — this is essential to a good aim."

Hitting a quarter at 30 to 40 yards may strain our credulity, but would not be an impossibility among men who had shot constantly from childhood. Furthermore, Miller realizes only too well that his statement can be questioned, for he emphasizes the importance these Snake Indians placed upon their arrows and the need for a calm day. At another place (p.189) he comments:

> "To the left in the sketch is seated an arrow-maker, busily engaged in preparing and pointing shafts, made usually from the Cottonwood tree, on account of its lightness, and being easily worked; — great care is taken in having the arrow well balanced, straight, and uniform throughout; — as on this depends the directness of its flight and aim" (Fig. 36).

It is customary for American writers to deride the fighting ability of the Mexicans in what is now the southwestern United States, conveniently forgetting the distance and deserts lying between Mexico City and Santa Fe. Bernardo De Galvez (1951) was in fact one of the most experienced and capable administrators ever to hold office under a European monarch on the American frontier. In 1786 Galvez set himself to the problem of reorganizing the defense of his far-flung northern provinces, and his conclusions were set down in explicit instructions to his various governors which completely reversed the long-held Spanish policy of keeping guns out of the hands of Indians. He states that, since it is impossible to defeat the Indians as long as they continue to use the bow, because of its superior firepower, every effort should be made to arm the hostiles with guns and thereby reduce the conflict to more even terms!

Anyone who has shot both the bow and the muzzle-loading rifle or fowling-piece is inevitably puzzled by the historic fact that the mountain men, usually in small groups and often in parties of only two or three, wandered almost at will over the plains and mountains of the West during the first half of the 19th Century. How could they do it in the face of hostile Indians on every hand?

Obviously, it was not their guns alone which gave them this advantage over the Indians, for it was not until the cap-and-ball revolver was introduced that the whites began to equal the Plains Indians in firepower. Until then the advantage of the whites lay in their relative freedom from superstition and the fact that they were not burdened with the hocus-pocus of making medicine before undertaking an engagement. In this respect, I will close this study of Native bows with a quotation from George Catlin (1857:I,33-4) who, writing just as the revolver reached the Plains, possibly touched without too much exaggeration upon one weakness in the Indians' armament.

"An Indian, therefore, mounted on a fleet and well-trained horse, with his bow in his hand, and his quiver slung on his back, containing an hundred arrows of which he can throw fifteen or twenty in a minute, is a formidable and dangerous enemy . . .

"In this wise then, are these wild knights of the prairie, armed and equipped . . . There can be no set of mounted men of equal numbers so effective and invincible in this country as they would be, could they be inspired with confidence of their own powers and their own superiority; yet this never can be done; — for the Indian, as far as the name of white man has travelled, and long before he has to try his strength with him, is trembling with fright and fear of his approach; he hears of the white man's arts and artifice — his tricks and cunning, and his hundred instruments of death and destruction — he dreads his approach, shrinks from him with fear and trembling — his heart sickens, and his pride and courage wither, at the thought of contending with an enemy, whom he thinks may war and destroy with weapons of *medicine* or mystery."

FIGURE 38. "Running Buffalo," a pencil sketch by Carl Wimar made on the Plains in 1859. Though the bow is indicated only by one expert line, the artist has caught the action of the chase perfectly. This underarm side shot could be made only with a short horse-bow, such as the reinforced or the American composite. *Missouri Historical Society.*

Figure 39. *The Buffalo Hunt* by Carl Wimar. Wimar made six trips up the Missouri, before making this oil painting in 1860, to study the Indians and make pencil sketches of buffalo hunts and other activities. Note particularly the horn bow, the draw, the release and the proper relationship in size of the pony to its rider. *Collection, Washington University, St. Louis, Missouri.*

Appendix I
On Making Horn Bows
by Bill Holm

1. FROM MOUNTAIN SHEEP HORN

There is something very exciting and romantic about the idea of a bow made of mountain sheep horn, short enough to be handily shot from a galloping horse and powerful enough to kill a buffalo. Early travelers and writers on the Plains mentioned them in glowing terms. In 1951, as an enthusiastic student of Indian culture and a moderately proficient archer, I was fascinated to the point of acquiring a big old ram horn and trying to make one. I had never knowingly seen a horn bow and knew nothing of the principles involved in their construction. I had seen lots of Plains sinew reinforced bows—in fact owned one which I occasionally shot—so I modeled my sheep horn bow after a double curved wooden bow and, in ignorance, substituted a rawhide back for the sinew reinforcement. The bow was made of two pieces spliced at the grip, was about 40 inches long by about 1¼ inches wide and ½ inch thick, and was embellished with a handsome strip of rattlesnake skin glued over the rawhide back. I thought it a very elegant bow (although of only about 30 pounds weight and of disappointing cast) until one day it almost literally exploded at full draw, leaving me with a lump on the head and pieces of sheep horn, rawhide and snakeskin spread around the countryside. I decided that the problem had been that the bow was made of old, long dried horn and vowed someday to make another and better one. I now believe that the bow broke because of the absence of sinew.

In anticipation of this project I began, in 1961, to make a fancy otterskin quiver and bowcase which reached a fair state of completion and then reposed in a closet until 1977 when, to my good fortune, I read T. M. Hamilton's book *Native American Bows*. The information on horn bows was a revelation. About the same time I had the opportunity to examine, photograph and measure a total of 14 old sheep horn bows. I had some horns and sinew available and couldn't wait to try another with my newfound knowledge.

The first one in the new series was intended as an experiment and was made of a single strip of horn about 34 inches long after straightening. With its heavy sinew back it was about ⅞ of an inch wide and ¾ of an inch thick. This little bow had an even curved reflex of about 4 inches. When braced it had a smooth "D" form. I made a tillering frame and drew and weighed the bow. I was amazed to draw this 30 inch (braced length) bow over 20 inches at which point it weighed 60 pounds! This seemed to be the real limit as the weight

FIGURE 40. An otterskin quiver and bowcase made by Bill Holm in the Crow–Nez Perce tradition, complete with bandolier.

suddenly increased to more than I could draw. I believe the sinew had reached the limit of its stretch.

The bow was very difficult for me to brace, partly because it was not quite straight as viewed from the back or belly and partly because it was narrow and tended to twist suddenly as the reflex was being taken up, unless held very tightly. This violent twist puts great stress on the horn. The bow had what seemed at the time to be the very unusual property of having one limb or the other slowly overwhelm its opposite until it was almost straight while the other increased its curve. On one occasion this continued until the bow suddenly reversed. The strain was so great that one limb was cracked straight across and nearly through the horn. I decided that, if the theory of the horn being in compression and the sinew in tension was correct, the bow should still function. I gingerly braced it, fastened it to the tillering frame and slowly brought it to a full draw—with no apparent change of form or weight!

Since the bow was experimental I proceeded to distress it to pieces, scraping and tillering, overdrawing and twisting, until I finally could only salvage the sinew. I found that tillering by scraping the horn thinner made surprisingly little difference, the stiffness of the limbs seemingly mainly dependent on the thickness of the sinew.

The excitement of making the sheephorn bow inspired the completion of the long delayed quiver project (Figure 40), and the next bow was begun. This one was made of two pieces spliced at the grip. The tapered lap is about 4 inches long and fastened with four copper rivets and glue. The splice could be less rugged as the primary force on it is compression. The bow (Figure 41) is 39 inches along the curve, 1 inch by ⅝ inch at the grip, ¹³⁄₁₆ by ½ inch at midlimb and ½ by ⅜ inch below the nocks, which are merely wrappings of sinew. When braced it is 35½ inches long. This bow also takes a while after bracing to stabilize, one limb or the other tending to straighten somewhat. I think it is this tendency which results in horn bows reversing while still strung, as seen in some old specimens. If the bow is left braced for hours the limbs lose some of their reflex curve when relaxed, but regain most of it within a few minutes and the rest of it in about thirty minutes as the sinew contracts.

This bow is very similar in dimension to a fine bow collected by Paul Kane in 1846 and now in the Manitoba Museum of Man and Nature in Winnipeg. Like the experimental bow this second bow is narrow, with a strong reflex, and is difficult to brace without twisting. Sure enough, a careless bracing allowed the bow to reverse suddenly and one limb cracked almost exactly as had the little test bow. (Figure 42) But as in that bow, there is not a sign of any effect on the bow's function or form. It weighs 55 pounds at the 22 inch maximum draw, at which point it stiffens. The outer layer of sinew

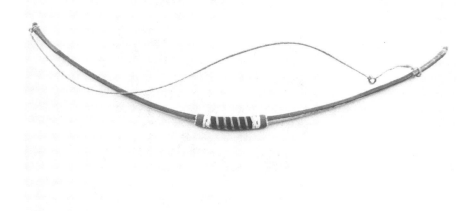

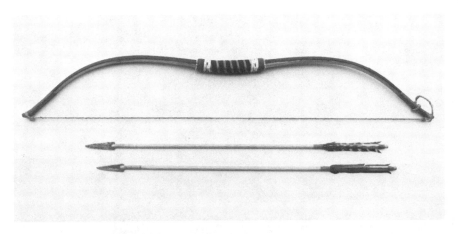

FIGURE 41. The second sheephorn bow made by Bill Holm, shown relaxed and braced. It is 39 inches long, measured along the curve, 1 x ⅝ inches at the grip, ¹³⁄₁₆ x ½ at midlimb and ½ x ⅝ below the nocks. When braced, it is 35½ inches long.

This bow weighs 55 pounds at full draw of 22 inches.

119

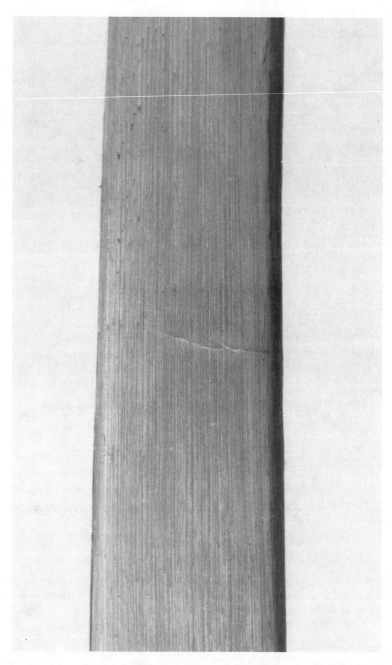

FIGURE 42. The crack in the belly of the bow after reversing itself while being braced. The horn and sinew were glued together and the bow still registers 55 pounds at 22 inches!

FIGURE 43. Bill Holm with the bow shown in Figure 41 at full draw. The sinew back stretches 1½ inches. The tips are wrapped with sinew in lieu of nocks to keep the bowstring from slipping off because the tips are not recurved.

The cast is 235 Yards using a Plains style arrow; not a flight arrow.

stretches 1½ inches over the length of the bow as measured relaxed and at full draw!

This little bow consistently shoots around 200 yards. My longest shots have been 235 yards. I find it hard to shoot at a target because I can't easily hold the 55 pounds at such a short draw. I'm sure such bows were ordinarily drawn and shot in one motion, rather than holding at full draw while aiming. Probably the draw length would be increased if the bow had less reflex.

One of the bows in the United States National Museum is particularly pleasing in form to me and I decided to make a one piece bow based on that model and record the process. After my previous three experiences in sawing the bow blank from the helical sheep horn on a band saw I decided that there had to be a better way! Sheep horn cuts beautifully on the saw, but the awkward shape of the massive horn makes it nearly impossible to control the direction of the cut or keep from binding the blade. This time, with a chisel and mallet I cut a deep V groove (Figure 44) the full length of both sides of the horn and then split it with wedges. The rough outer surface was easily cut smooth with a light hatchet. The horn is somewhat brittle and the sharp edged chips fly fast and hard, so some eye protection is in order. The horn strip was thinned on its inner surface (Figure 45) with the hatchet to somewhat more than the final thickness. It's important to cut the final strip in such a way that the bow is as straight as possible, so I laid a strip of tape around the horn as a guide and cut the horn strip to width (Figure 46) with a hand saw. Careful chopping would do nearly as well. Next the helical (Figure 47) horn strip was boiled about 30 minutes, straightened and tied to a board to cool and dry. At this point it had a slight reflex curve and could be easily worked to final thickness and width. The horn was sawn and then scraped with a knife (which works beautifully) to a width of 1¼ inches at the grip, tapering to 7/16 inch at the tips. The thickness of the horn is 5/16 at the grip tapering to ¼ inch at the tips. The horn was scraped to a cross section which was nearly flat on the back (Figure 48) and somewhat rounded on the belly.

The next step was to bring the horn to its final form by heating and bending. My previous experiments showed that the drying sinew increased the reflex considerably, so the horn was shaped straighter than its anticipated final form. The thinner and more flexible the horn, the greater this reflexing effect. Sheep horn is quite easy to form with heat. Boiling water is convenient and quite adequate as a heat source. I did my shaping (Figure 49) in a cake pan. The center of the horn was immersed in the boiling water for about 5 minutes, or enough to thoroughly heat it clear through, and then quickly bent to a shape a bit beyond the planned form and held in that shape under cold water until chilled. A little extra reflex at the grip helps to achieve the "double curved" form when braced. The limbs were then boiled and formed one at a time in the

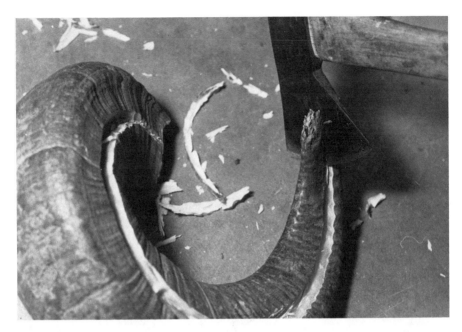

FIGURE 44. Cutting the grooves on each side of the horn before splitting it with wedges.

FIGURE 45. Thinning the inner surface of the horn with a hatchet.

123

FIGURE 46. The strip of tape used as a guide so the horn strip will cut out straight.

FIGURE 47. The strip of horn before boiling.

FIGURE 48. Final shaping of the horn belly by scraping.

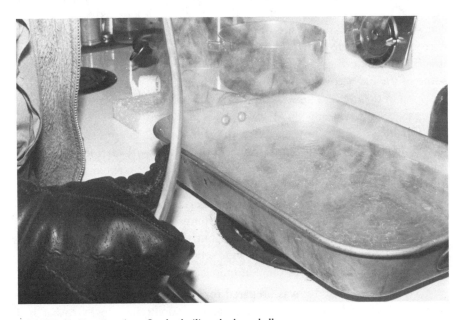

FIGURE 49. Forming the reflex by boiling the horn belly.

same manner, shaping them to a somewhat flatter reflex than desired. The tip end of the sheep horn is harder to form than the rest of it. It needs more heat and overbending to achieve the desired form. Some old horn bows have a reflexed double curve form. I believe they were shaped as double curved bows and the shrinking sinew back produced the reflex. Finally the sharply recurved tips were easily formed by boiling just the tips and bending with a pair of pliers.

My first two sinew back bows were made with elk sinew. The third bow uses mule deer sinew. I used only the back sinew, at first because that's what I had, and later, after I had some leg sinew, because I liked it better. It's longer and much easier to shred. Neck sinew is useless. It is very brittle when dry and will not shred. Back sinew is very easy to work with and is such an interesting material that using it affords a lot of satisfaction. The sinews lie in very thin, flat bands just under the muscle layer on each side of and parallel to the spine. They are quite easily separated from the surrounding muscles with the fingers. They should be thoroughly scraped free of any clinging muscle and fat and washed. Laid out flat they will dry in a few hours to a stiff, thin sheet. On one face the sinew strip is covered with a thin paperlike fascia which can be removed by scraping or by working the sinew until it loosens. Shredding the sinew for bow backing is simply a matter of splitting it with the fingers to narrow strands. Before applying, it is soaked in water. An hour in warm water is sufficient. Sinew can be softened very quickly by chewing, as described in some of the old accounts. Saliva seems to penetrate it very fast, aided by the working of the fibers. This technique is most useful if a small amount of sinew needs to be softened quickly.

On the first two bows I glued the sinew with commercial hide glue, heated in a double boiler and applied hot. That worked fine, but I was interested in the native preparation of glues so experimented with boiling salmon skin and buffalo hide scrapings. Both were successful. The last bow was made with buffalo hide glue. The scrapings were boiled for about 5 hours, adding water from time to time. The scrapings don't melt into glue, as one might anticipate from written accounts, but the water becomes thicker and browner as it boils, and the kettle of hide scrapings produced just enough fine hide glue, nearly identical to the commercial product, to attach the sinew.

The back of the bow was prepared for the sinew and glue by scratching (Figure 50) rather deeply with the back of a knife point, in a close crosshatched pattern. With glue pot and wet sinew handy I clamped the bow in place and wet the back thoroughly with hot water to soften the surface and clean away any oil. Then I laid a thin coat of hot glue on the grip area and one limb. Holding a strand of sinew in one hand I pinched it between thumbnail and finger of the other hand and scraped it flat. Then I dipped it in the hot glue

FIGURE 50. Crosshatching the back of the belly in preparation for the glue and sinew.

FIGURE 51. Applying the sinew-in-glue back to the horn belly.

(kept quite thin by adding water from time to time), held it up over the pot and stripped the hot glue the length of the strand before placing the thicker end on the grip of the bow and laying the strand right up the limb. (Figure 51) The glue must be kept somewhat below boiling, or the sinew will shrivel up and be useless. Elk and big mule deer back sinews will reach across the grip, up the limb and over the end onto the belly of such a short bow.

After placing, the sinew strand was smoothed and flattened into place with the finger. This process was repeated, laying the strands carefully alongside one another until the entire limb and grip were covered. The process was repeated for the other limb. The overlapping at the grip somewhat stiffens it. One or two layers of sinew can be laid in place before the bow is set aside to dry.

The hide glue sets up to a jelly-like consistency as it cools. The sinew must be in good contact as it takes a few hours for the sinew and glue to dry, and as it dries, the sinew shrinks. On a reflexed back the shrinking tends to pull the sinew away from the horn. This problem is most acute at the area of greatest reflex, the grip. Some bowmakers are said to have wrapped the drying bow with bark. I experimented with a strip of canvas which worked fairly well if the glue was allowed to set up somewhat before wrapping. On the third bow I used a strip of nylon net, tightly wrapped over the drying sinew. In good drying conditions a single layer of glue and sinew dries enough in about a day so that new layers can be added.

I allowed two full days drying before bending the bow. The sinew continues to shrink over many months, increasing the reflex. A little sinew goes a long way for power. This little bow would probably have weighed 15 pounds if I had dared draw it before backing. With five layers of sinew it weighs over 50 pounds at a 20 inch draw! It is $7/16$ inch thick at the grip and $3/8$ inch thick below the nock. Approximately $1/3$ of this thickness is sinew. (Figure 52)

After the sinew layers were all in place to my satisfaction, the grip and ends were wrapped with glued sinew and "nocks" were formed by wrapping sinew around each end below the recurved tips. A tight wrapping of buckskin at the grip completed this bow. The other one is more elaborate. The sinew back is painted black, the end wrappings vermilion, and the grip covered with blue and red stroud, plaited porcupine quill wrapping, buckskin thong and beaded edging, all sewn with sinew.

The bowstrings are of three ply twisted sinew. I have a fixed loop at each end, one end fastened firmly and the other attached loosely with a buckskin tie. I usually sit down to brace. I put one tip behind my left knee with my right knee against the belly at the grip. Holding the lower limb tightly with my left hand, I bend the upper limb toward me with my right hand until the loop can be slipped over the tip with my left hand. The bow must be firmly held while

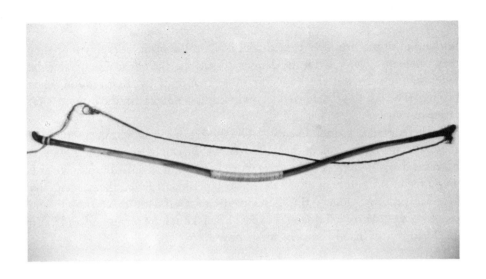

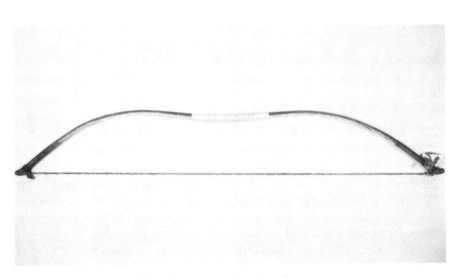

FIGURE 52. The completed bow shown relaxed and braced.

This bow has five layers of sinew in its back and weighs 50 pounds at 20 inches of draw. It is $7/16$ inches thick at the grip and $3/8$ at the nocks. Approximately $1/3$ of the thickness of the bow is sinew.

bending until the tips have passed well beyond the plane of the grip or they may suddenly reverse, with the danger of cracking the horn. The greater the reflex or the narrower the bow, the more chance of twisting around when bracing. The last bow, being wider and with less reflex than the others, is far easier to brace.

These little bows look like toys. The shorter one is only 32 inches overall, about average for mountain sheep horn bows. It weighs just 8 ounces, but its power is truly impressive. The sheep horn bow is not as difficult to make as it might seem. A number of others have also experimented with them, including Norman Feder of Sidney, B.C., Reginald Laubin of Moose, Wyoming, and Jack Contor of Fort Hall, Idaho. I expect I'll make at least one more, and I also intend to try my hand at an elk antler bow.

2. FROM ELK ANTLER

After completing the two successful mountain sheep horn bows the desire to tackle an elk antler bow became too strong to resist, in spite of other pressing responsibilities which good sense indicated should take precedence. These were fairly easily shunted aside when I checked through my pile of antler scraps and found one twenty inch piece of a big antler beam. After eyeing this short section it seemed that with careful placement the two limbs could be cut from the single piece. I had hoped to try a one piece bow, as some were certainly made that way, but I hadn't been able to find a suitable antler, so with the short piece available the spliced bow was the only possibility. It would give me a bow of 36 inches, close to the average length of the antler bows I've seen. The bow carried by Pehriska Ruhpa in Carl Bodmer's famous watercolor of the chief, in Dog Dance dress, looks to be about that length.

Antler is quite easy to work, being somewhat softer than sheep horn, but it is more brittle, much stiffer and very much more difficult to alter in shape by boiling. In fact it is important to lay out the bow stave carefully to utilize the natural curves of the antler as much as possible. With a spliced bow this is a relatively simple matter—with a one piece bow it would be very difficult to achieve the proper shape without bending. If the antler bowstave is soaked in water for several days it can be bent fairly easily after a few minutes of boiling or steaming. There are ways of softening antler so that difficult bends can be made, but I wanted to use techniques available to 19th century Indian craftsmen. By setting that period as my era of bowmaking I left myself the option of utilizing trade cloth and beads for decoration and, most importantly, the use of a steel hatchet! This turned out to be the principal tool used in shaping the limbs.

Unlike the coiled sheep horn, elk antler is simple to saw on a bandsaw, but I decided to use that tool only to split my antler piece. If I hadn't needed both halves it would have been a simple matter to chop the limb from the solid antler. Since Gilbert Wilson's description of antler bow making mentioned chopping tines off with a butcher knife, I decided to try that tool to see how practical it was. With little effort I chopped through an antler beam with a diameter of one and three quarter inches in just over five minutes with an old trade butcher knife. The hatchet took less than a minute for the same job.

The antler I used was a big one, with a maximum diameter of just over two inches. The solid outer wall was about one quarter of an inch thick. Chopping each limb to shape with the hatchet took about a half an hour—the two limbs were chopped out, scraped to shape and spliced in one afternoon. An evening spent with the boiling pan produced the minimal bends I needed to begin the sinewing. I found I just could not sharply recurve the tips, a detail that is very important for these very short bows, and which is simple to do with sheep horn. When fully drawn (about 22 inches) the string leaves the nocks at an obtuse angle. Without some kind of hook at the tip there is a good chance for the string to slip off the nock, which very likely would result in the bow's destruction as well as (in earlier days) the loss of a buffalo or the archer's scalp! My solution was to build up a little knob of sinew on the back of each tip.

The sinewing procedure was exectly as with the horn bows, except that the slightly porous inner surface of the antler (the last vestige of the core) furnished a ready-made gluing surface, supplementing the scratched texture. However the effect of the drying sinew on the antler bow was entirely different from that on the horn bows. After a year of drying the reflex has hardly changed, whereas the sheep horn bows have radically increased in reflex. The small antler bow performed quite similarly to the little one piece horn bow, although I haven't tested them objectively.

It is clear that, in spite of Catlin's doubts, elk antler bows were made and are entirely practical. I know of fourteen in museums and private collections. In some respects an antler bow is simpler to make than a sheep horn bow, although each material has its own problems as well as its advantages and beauties.

Some time after the antler bow was finished one limb was broken clear through in three places, as could be expected when the bow was drawn backwards by a visitor. Unfortunately I wasn't present to warn him. I decided to reglue the sinew where it had separated from the antler and glue up the broken surfaces. After drying, the bow shows no change in shape when drawn, but I haven't worked up the nerve to shoot it since!

Bert Grayson, of Clatskanie, Oregon, has made a beautiful antler bow as well as several sheep horn bows. He uses Le Page's liquid glue for his sinewing, rather than hot hide glue, with excellent results.

I have gleaned additional comments on horn bows from Mr. Holm's letters as follows: [TMH]

I used the outside of the horn for the belly in all three sinew back bows. I'm quite sure that that is true for those old ones I have examined. A very careful examination could settle it since the grain of the horn runs more and more diagonally through it toward the base, and the direction of this slant would determine whether the outer or inner part of the horn stave appears on the belly. I'm quite sure it's done the way I did it.

The sinew on my bows goes up the back, over the end and down on the belly several inches, or at least far enough to be siezed under the nock wrapping and then some. Since I wrapped all of them for several inches on each end with sinew the ends on the belly are covered and not visible. Actually, not every strand of sinew goes over the end, but on the shorter bow at least, most do.

I don't find it too hard to bend the bow, at least the smaller one which is far easier to brace, and then tie the string. I haven't been doing that because I find the loop much more convenient. I suppose in the interest of authenticity I should tie the string, just as I should get used to the Indian form of release.

My little bow does not ripple nearly as badly as the longer. One limb seems a little straighter than the other, but I find that I can "set" them so they are symmetrical by grasping the weaker limb and string together for about a minute and then the bow will remain symmetrical for as long as braced.

Norm Feder thinks that all elk antler bows are one piece, but I am sure I know of at least one and maybe two that are two piece. One of those in the Smithsonian is clearly one piece, but the others are wrapped at the grip and it isn't at all clear. Norm has examined more elkhorn bows than I have however. I think I will make mine two piece, since I know of at least one for certain. However I had an elk antler (since cut up for other projects, however) that I'm sure could have made a nice one piece bow. The antlers vary considerably in the amount and direction of bends, so I think that the right antler could be found to use for a one piece bow. I agree that it is much easier to get big antlers which have been shed than to find useable sheep horns. Sheep horns do turn up, however, mostly on old motheaten trophies.

I was just looking at Payne-Gallwey, *Projectile Throwing Engines of the Ancients with a treatise on the Turkish and Other Oriental Bows* and he is very definite on the use of neck sinew in Turkish bows. He also says that if the sinew is soaked apart it is in short pieces. I wasn't able to use neck sinew at all. It was completely worthless. I got a great box of it from a slaughterhouse, thinking that I would have enough sinew to last a lifetime, and I threw it *all* out!

132

Appendix II
From the Grayson Collection

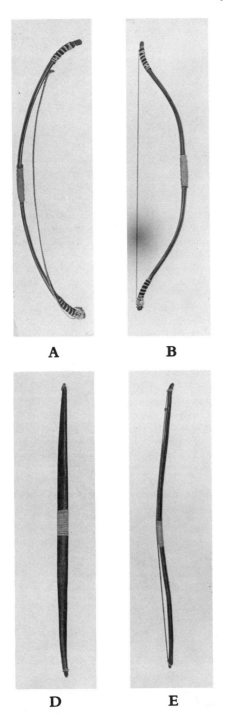

A   **B**

C

FIGURE 53. Horn Bows from the Grayson Collection. A and B. An old mountain sheep horn bow, rebuilt by Dr. Grayson, shown relaxed and braced. It was in extremely poor condition when found and has some lateral curvature, but is now usable.

C. The above bow at full draw. Weight 65 pounds. It is 42 inches long and measures 1½ by ⅝ inches just above the center splice. The arrow shown is 28 inches long.

D and E. A sheephorn bow, 32½ inches long, 1¼ wide and 9/16 thick just above the center wrapping. This bow is an old one made of one piece of mountain sheep horn with the sinew back covered with pitch. It has the original sinew string and is in such good condition that no repair work was required. A few flakes of pitch are missing due to excessive drying.

The sinew is probably no more than ⅛ inch thick. The sinew goes over the bow tips to form a slight notch and the tips are wrapped with sinew.

D   **E**

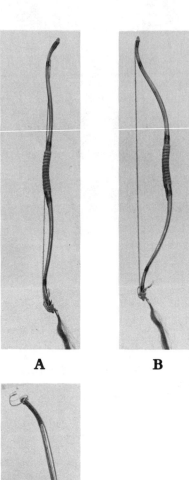

A   B

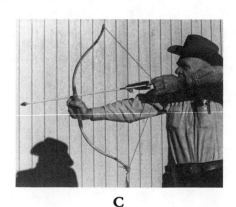

C

D

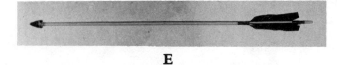

E

FIGURE 54. Horn Bows from the Grayson Collection. A and B. This sheephorn bow was made in 1981 by Dr. Grayson. It is shown relaxed and braced.

C. The above bow at full draw. At 22 inches its weight is 60 pounds. Full length of bow is 37 inches and it measures 1¼ x ¾ inches just above the center splice. The sinew back is from ⅛ to 3/16 inches in thickness.

D. An elkhorn bow made by Dr. Grayson in 1981. It is 44 inches long and measures 1 1/16 x ⅝ inches just above the center splice.

E. One of a half dozen arrows made by Dr. Grayson in the Plains Indian fashion from the snow berry bush. Shaft heat straightened and scraped. The points were made from flint and obsidion chipped using a deer antler tine and secured with a wrapping of sinew coated with pitch for waterproofing, as are the backs of his bows.

"The feathers are from the tail of a Florida wild turkey, shot with a bow, though I didn't get it myself".

Appendix III

A. ACTUAL BOW PERFORMANCES

The pioneering work in the study of native American bows was done by Saxton Pope from about 1918 to 1924. His various studies listed in the reference section cannot be too highly recommended. The following tabulation, with the exception of the first two flight records made by Turks and included for comparative purposes, has been extracted from the writings of Saxton Pope. Unless otherwise noted under "comments," all information listed can be found in his STUDY IN BOWS AND ARROWS (republished in 1962 under the title BOWS AND ARROWS). It is here presented through the courtesy of the University of California Press.

In comparing the casts of the various bows, several factors must be carefully weighed. First, a distinction must be drawn between the performances of the replicas and those of the aged Indian bows. On the other hand, the casts of these ancient bows were undoubtedly helped tremendously by the efficiency of the flight arrows used throughout the test. In short, the cast of the flight arrow is so much greater than that of the aboriginal arrow that, in most instances, it more than cancelled out any disadvantages due to age. This, however, is a matter of opinion and cannot be reduced to a formula.

Particular attention is called to the performance of the replica of the bow stave taken from the hulk of the "Mary Rose," sunk in the year 1545 off the coast of England and recovered in 1841 (Pope, 1923:351). As a rough stave 76-3/4 inches long it weighed only 52 pounds at 28 inches of draw and cast the flight arrow only 185 yards. By drawing a special flight arrow 36 inches, Pope got a cast of 212 yards. Substituting a replica of an Old English war arrow and drawing it 36 inches, the cast dropped to 117 yards.

Undoubtedly, Pope also checked the cast of the war arrow at a practical draw of 28 inches. It is unfortunate that he made no record of that cast, but it obviously was too low to be of effective field use.

By reducing the length of this stock stave to 72 inches, the weight at 28 inches jumped to 62 pounds and the cast to 227 yards. A further reduction in length to 68 inches, with appropriate tillering, put the weight up to 70 pounds and a cast of 245 yards with the flight arrow.

The Paraguay bow shows dramatically how proper tillering will improve the cast of many native bows.

Fortunately for us, Pope was in a position which enabled him to make these tests. And, since Pope drew upon three bow collections — from the University of California, the Jessop, and the American Museum of Natural History — there seems to be little reason to pursue such tests further. As was characteristic of the man, when Pope tested these bows he did it thoroughly.

In checking the cast of any given group of bows it is obvious that the same arrow must be used throughout the test. It would be well if a uniform length of draw could be used also, but this is impractical since, with primitive bows, the one with the shortest draw would limit the cast of all the others.

In these tests which follow, Pope used flight arrows which Ishi made expressly for that purpose. According to Pope (1923 A:333):

> "Two shafts made by Ishi of bamboo, having a birch foreshaft and very low-cropped feathers, have repeatedly proved themselves the best flyers. They will carry ten percent farther than the best English flight arrow, and twenty percent farther than the standard target arrow weighing 435 grains. These bamboo flight arrows, therefore, have been used in all our tests. One is 29 inches in length, the other 25 inches. The former weighs 310 grains, the latter 200 grains. They are feathered with soft turkey feathers, clipped as close as is compatible with steering requirements."

As we have said, the use of these exceedingly efficient flight arrows compensates for the age of the bows. As Pope again observes (1923 A:332), "The average native arrow is a crude contrivance and is illy calculated to fly far or straight."

Pope's comments (1923 A:333) on the length of draw used in the tests is as follows:

> "The average Indian bow, however, is obviously constructed to draw less than 28 inches. This fact, and a study of their arrows and the bending capacity of their bows, will convince any archer that 25 or 26 inches is the average draw of most natives. Wherever possible, therefore, we shot the longer arrows on the tested bows, drawing them till a sense of resistance warned of impending fracture of the bow, then released. In the very short bows we shot only the short arrow. All bows were shot repeatedly, at least six times, over the same ground on calm days. The distance was measured with a tape and marked off in ten-yard sections.
>
> "The attempt in every test was to get out of the bow all the cast that was in it. No implement was spared out of respect for its age or apparent infirmity . . .
>
> "The elevation at which each arrow was projected was approximately 45 degrees from the horizontal. A quick release was given upon full draw . . . the greatest distance was recorded as the full capacity of each bow."

Finally, they used both the Tertiary and Mediterranean releases with "no apparent difference in the cast of the bows dependent upon these conditions."

TABULATION OF BOW PERFORMANCES

Tribe, etc.	Material & Type	Length, inches	Dimensions: Grip Mid-Limb Below nocks	Draw, inches	Weight, pounds	Cast, yards	Comments
Turkish flight bow	Composite	?	?	?	?	482	By Mamhood Effendij in 1795 (Klopsteg, p. 2)
Turkish flight bow	Composite	?		?	?	972	Sultan Selim, 1798, (Klopsteg, p. 3)
English target bow	Yew?	?	?	28?	48	220	Imported (Pope, 1923 B, p. 44)
English yew flight bow	Yew	?	?	28?	65	300	(Pope, 1923 B, p. 44)
Old English longbow, hunting	Oregon yew	68	1-1/4 x 1-1/8 / 1-1/8 x 7/8 / 5/8 x 5/8	28	75	250	Replica by Pope.
Composite flight bow	Composite, catgut back	48	? / 1-1/4 x 3/4	29	85	274	Replica by Pope. Special 30" flight arrow.
English longbow stave	Oregon yew	76-3/4	4-1/2" circum. / 4" circum. / ?	28 / 36 / 36	52 / 72 / 72	185 / 212 / 117	Replica by Pope of "Mary Rose" stave. Shooting English war arrow.
The above stave	Oregon yew	72	? / ? / ?	28	62	227	Above cut down. Regular flight arrow again used.
The same stave	Oregon yew	68	?	28	70	245	Again cut down. Same flight arrow.
Sudbury bow, Peabody Museum	Red hickory	67-1/4	1-3/16 x 15/16 / 9/16 x 1-3/4 / 3/8 x 3/4	28	46	173	Replica by Pope. Dimensions by Dr. Greengo.
Alaskan	Douglas fir, sinew-corded	56	1-1/2 x 3/4 / ? / 1 x 5/8	26	80	180	Eskimo bow.

TABULATION OF BOW PERFORMANCES (Continued)

Tribe, etc.	Material & Type	Length, inches	Dimensions: Grip Mid-Limb Below nocks	Draw, inches	Weight, pounds	Cast, yards	Comments
Apache, double curved	White hickory. Wagon hoop. Sinew-backed	41	1-5/8 x 1-5/8 7/8 x 1/2 5/8 x 3/8	22	28	120	Native arrow 24" long. Flight arrow used.
Blackfoot, slight reflex, no backing	Ash?	47-1/2	1-3/8 x 3/4 1-1/4 x 9/16 3/4 x 3/8	25	45	145	Poor shooter. Bucked in hand.
Blackfoot, reflexed	Red hickory, sinew-backed	40	1-3/8 x 5/8 1-1/4 x 1/2 3/4 x 1/2	20	40	153	Buffalo bow. Sweet shooter.
Cheyenne	Ash, sinew-backed	45	1-1/4 x 7/8 1-1/8 x 3/4 7/8 x 5/8	20 24	65 80	156 ?	
Cree	Ash	44	1-5/8 x 1/2 1-3/8 x 7/16 1 x 3/8	20	38	150	Broke at 20" draw.
Hupa, strong reflex	Yew, sinew-backed	47	1-1/2 x 1/2 2-1/4 x 3/8 7/8 x 7/16	22	40	148	Bends in center. Bucks in hand.
Luiseno	Willow	55-1/2	1-1/2 x 3/4 1-1/2 x 5/8 1 x 1/2	26	48	125	Jarring recoil. Poor weapon.
Navajo	Mesquite, sinew-backed	44	1 x 3/4 7/8 x 5/8 1/2 x 1/2	26	45	150	Well-made. Tillered.
Mohave	Willow	67	1-3/8 x 1 1-1/8 x 3/4 3/4 x 1/2	28	40	110	Whip-ended. Flabby cast.
Osage	Osage orange	47-1/2	7/8 x 7/8 1-1/2 x 1/2 5/8 x 3/8	20	40	92	Poor bow for wood used.

Name	Material	Length	Dimensions			Notes
Sioux	?	?	?	?	45	165	(Pope, 1923B p. 43)
South American	Palma Brava	74	7/8 x 5/8 3/4 x 1/2 1/2 x 3/8	28	50	98	Slow action. Bad design.
Tomawata	?	?	?	?	40	148	(Pope, 1923B, p. 43)
Yurok, reflexed	Yew, sinew-backed	54	1-7/8 x 1/2 2 x 3/8 1 x 3/8	28	30	140	Bends at grip. Flabby cast. Bucks.
Yukon, with bridge	Birch	68	1-1/2 x 1 1-3/8 x 3/4 1 x 1/2	25	60	125	Twists in hand. Poor shooter.
Yaqui	Osage orange	59-1/2	1-1/2 x 7/8 1-1/4 x 5/8 1 x 3/8	28	70	210	Best bow tested.
Yana, slightly recurved	Red yew, rawhide-backed	55	1-5/8 x 5/8 1-3/4 x 1/2 3/4 x 3/8	28	48	205	An Ishi bow. Excellent workmanship.
Paraguay	Ironwood?	71	1-1/4 x 1 1-1/2 x 7/8 9/16 x 3/8	25	60	170	Poor workmanship Excellent wood.
Same bow retillered	Ironwood?	67	?	28	85	265	Regular flight arrow used.
Same bow unchanged	Ironwood?	67	?	28	85	276	Special flight arrow with reduced feathers.

Appendix IV

B. DESCRIPTIONS OF TEN HORN BOWS
IN UNITED STATES NATIONAL MUSEUM

Dr. Waldo R. Wedel, former curator of the Division of American Archaeology, Smithsonian Institution, undertook to furnish descriptions of the ten horn bows now in the National Museum, and George Metcalf, at that time aide in the Division of American Archaeology, made the measurements and wrote the descriptions.

Because of their rarity it is felt that the descriptions of these specimens should be made a matter of record in this appendix. Where Metcalf's exact wording is used, quotation marks are shown. The brackets enclose my wording inserted to give continuity to the condensation of Metcalf's descriptions.

Catalogue No. 154015. Sioux. Metcalf upon examining the bow says that it must actually be made of cow horn and that it definitely is not bison horn. Over-all length is 34-1/2 inches. The other dimensions are: grip, 1-1/8 inches wide by 3/4 thick; mid-limb, 1-1/16 x 17/32; below nock, 7/16 x 3/8. The sinew thicknesses are 3/8 and 1/4 inches at grip and mid-limb respectively. It was impossible to determine sinew thickness at the nock. The sinew backing runs full length of bow.

"The bow is now broken in the center enabling one to see how the splice is made. In splicing it the two limbs were butted together and then riveted, with two iron rivets, to a short piece of horn about 8 inches long and placed on the back of the bow. One rivet appears to be 3/16 inches in diameter and to have been filed off smooth with the horn. The short splicing section of the horn is now broken."

This bow appears to have seen use.

Catalogue No. 6326 is a Gros Ventre [Hidatsa] bow received at the museum in July of 1868. The material again appears to be cow horn.

Over-all length is 36 inches. Dimensions are, grip, 1-3/16 x 3/4 inches; mid-limb 1 x 9/16; below nock, 7/16 x 7/16 [round]. The sinew thickness, as nearly as it can be determined, appears to account for half the thickness of the bow. In other words, the sinew seems to be about 3/8, 9/32, and 7/32 inches thick, respectively, at the three points of measurement.

This bow is also "spliced at the center by lapping one piece over the other and riveting. Eight rivets were used. Holes were drilled for the rivets and there is some cracking here, either due to strain or to the pounding on the rivets, or both. The horn seems to have thinned here [at the center], and as with the first bow, the sinew extends well down the sides of the bow, and in an occasional place it comes down almost even with the face ... The overlap at the splice seems to be about

3-3/4 inches, but I can't be sure. The rivet placement suggests that it is only about 2-1/2 inches. This sounds confusing, I know, but the sinew comes down over the sides of the bow.

"This bow has warped somewhat, the two curves are uneven and it has twisted until the string is even with the side of the bow. In spite of that, it looks like a good job and still retains considerable spring."

Catalogue No. 8419 is an Arikara bow collected around 1870. It is of elk horn and is now crooked and badly warped. Over-all length is 39 inches, the grip measures 1-1/32 x 9/16; mid-limb, 7/8 x 1/2 and 1 x 7/16, below nock, 7/16 x 1/4. Sinew thickness at grip is 9/32 inches and 2 inches below the nock it is 3/32 inches thick. The sinew extends the full length of the bow and the nocks are cut into the horn.

Catalogue No. 154014 is Sioux. It also is of cow horn. This bow has no bowstring and it is sharply reflexed. The over-all length is 32 inches. The heavy sinew back is covered with canvas, which also covers approximately 4-1/2 inches of the belly side of the limb tips. Because of this canvas covering it is difficult to get exact measurements, but it is torn at a spot 6-3/4 inches from the limb end (or 1-1/4 from mid-limb). At this point the limb measures 5/8 x 1/2 inch thick. Of this limb thickness of 1/2 inch, 3/16 appears to be of horn and the remaining 5/16 is sinew. At 13 inches from the end of the limb (and 3 inches short of center of bow) the width is exactly 1 inch; the horn itself accounting for 13/16 and the remaining 3/16 is made up of sinew and canvas. The belly-to-back dimension at this point is not given. Below the nock the dimensions are 7/16 by 1/2 inch thick.

Catalogue No. 287128 is a Crow bow. It is made of a single piece of elk horn and where the sinew is loose on the back, it can be seen that the elk horn was gashed with cross-hatched cuts approximately 1/3 inch apart, apparently to give the glue which held the sinew to the back better footing. The interior of the antler became the back of this bow. It is badly broken at three places. "One near the center and at each end, 4-1/2 and 5 inches from the tips. Each of the broken parts is still attached to the sinew to which it was not only glued, but is also neatly and rather heavily wrapped with sinew thread. There are no nocks."

The over-all length is 40 inches. "This bow is much more flattened in cross section than the earlier ones I have described. I cannot give middle grip measurements accurately, but at 18-1/2 inches from the end it is 1 inch wide and 17/32 thick. At the point near this where it is broken (17 inches from end) the dimensions are only minutely less and here the horn is 7/8 inches wide and 3/8 thick. [This indicates a sinew thickness at this point of about 5/32 inches.] At mid-limb the width is 13/16 inches; the antler measuring 11/16 wide; the thickness is 15/32. At one break, 5-1/4 inches from the end, the bow is 5/8 inches wide and 7/16 thick. Here the antler is 1/2 inch wide and 5/32 thick. [This indicates a sinew thickness at this point of 9/32 inches. The last 1-1/2 or 2 inches of the limb-end is round.] At the other end the break is 4-1/2 inches from the end. Here the measurements of the bow (antler and sinew) are, width 5/8 inches, thickness 1/2 . . .

"This bow, in spite of mistreatment, has been a fine job; shows plenty of use, the wrapping at center is old, worn and dirty."

Catalogue No. 203812 is a Ute bow made of horn, probably mountain sheep. From Metcalf's comments this bow is apparently still braced and has reversed itself in its string, since the bowstring knots are still in their proper positions on the belly side. The horn is in a single piece and is 38 inches over all. The dimensions at grip are 1-5/16 x 3/4 inches; at mid-limb, 31/32 x 11/16; below nock, 9/16 x 15/32. "It is impossible to measure always the thickness of the horn and of the sinew, but it very definitely *looks* as if the horn was thinnest at the center, or grip, and the sinew correspondingly thicker at that point. At mid-limb the horn has a thickness of 11/32 inches, but at center [the grip] it looks no thicker. In fact it *looks* thinner. Backing goes to the very tips of the stave and the last 3 to 3-1/2 inches of the bow, at each end, is wrapped with fine sinew. . . . Two arrows are with this bow. No foreshafts. Small stone points. Remains of 3 feathers. On one 4-1/2 inches between sinew wrappings [holding feathers], on the other 6 inches. The arrow lengths are 23-5/8 and 22 inches. The short arrow has the longest feathers."

Since these arrows have been kept with this bow and everything indicates that they were collected with the bow, it seems that we are justified in assuming that they were intended to be used with it. This gives us a maximum draw of 23 inches for a 38-inch bow, or bow-draw ratio of 1.65 to 1!

Catalogue No. 14526 is a Pai-Ute bow collected by Major J.W. Powell, former director of the Bureau of Ethnology, Smithsonian Institution. It is still braced, has the cupid-bow shape, and still has enough tension on the cord for it to "hum slightly when plucked." It appears to be made of elk horn. The over-all length is 33-1/2 inches. The dimensions are: at grip 1-1/32 x 5/8 inches; mid-limb, 7/8 x 5/8; below nock, 17/32 x 1/2. "Sinew backing extends to tips. Short distance of fine sinew wrapping at end seems designed to aid nock in keeping bow string from slipping. Bow is wrapped with a thin, ribbon-like band of sinew for its entire length. This is tight, but irregularly spaced, sometimes overlapping and at other times with an inch or more between coils, although a quarter-inch is more usual. I find it impossible to estimate the sinew thickness, as with the Plains bows, the sinew has been molded well down the sides of the bow. This looks as if it had been a good bow. Undoubtedly had plenty of use. I would guess sinew was at least as thick as the horn."

Catalogue No. 14521 is a Pai-Ute bow also collected by Major Powell. "I think it is cow horn. I believe it is spliced in the middle but I can't be sure, nor can I tell how it was done, nor give true measurements of the bow at the center [because of the wrappings which cover the grip] . . . Bow is now, unstrung, a smooth curve with the sinew on the inside of the curve. No real nock is present, but from 3/8 to 1/2 inch from tips there is an abrupt taper, with a buckskin band immediately below."

The over-all length is 30 inches. Dimensions are: at edge of grip wrappings (or 12 inches from the tip), 1-1/32 x 5/8 inches; at mid-limb (7-1/2 from tip), 29/32 x 15/32; below nock (buckskin band 1 inch from tip), 15/32 x 15/32 inches. The sinew backing runs to the very tips. The sinew thickness at edge of grip wrappings is 9/32; at mid-limb, 1/4; and at nock, 1/8.

Catalogue No. 11219 was collected by Major Powell from the Pai-Ute. It is broken in the center and in poor condition. "I think this is horn, probably mountain sheep. Now bent in an arc, with sinew on inside of curve. Sinew extends slightly beyond the horn and is then bent sharply. No sign of a nock, but this bending, plus some wrapping probably formed the nock. [It] has been rather closely wrapped with a wide, thin, ribbon-like band of sinew on both limbs. Much of this is now gone, but stains indicate it extended from one-half to two-thirds of each limb. Ends are stained black with some material which looks like dried tar — perhaps pitch. This seems to have been used to fasten the sinew backing to the horn. A patch of this is present near the break in the center and carries string imprints."

The over-all length is 33 inches. The present tip-to-tip distance is 27 inches. The dimensions are: center of grip, 1-1/16 x 9/16; mid-limb (8-1/4 inches from tip), 15/16 x 1/2; 1 inch below tip, 1/2 x 9/32. The thickness of the sinew backing at center of grip is 5/16 inches. It was impossible to measure sinew thickness at the other points.

Catalogue No. 1882 represents a horn bow collected from the Digger Indians in California. It appears to be made of mountain sheep horn and has no string. This bow is sharply reflexed. "Sinew neatly fastened, nice workmanlike job of bow-making. Again, there are no nocks, and tips are somewhat bent back and a band of fine sinew forms a guard about an inch below the tip to prevent the string from slipping down the stave. Full sinew backed and a bit more. A thin ribbon-like strip of sinew is wound tightly around and around the bow from one end to the other so closely that the horn can only be seen occasionally."

The over-all length of the bow is 33 inches. The tip-to-tip distance is 29-1/2. The dimensions are: center of grip, 15/16 wide x 17/32 thick; mid-limb (8-1/4 inches from the tip), 7/8 x 7/16; below the nock band (1-3/8 inches from tip), 15/32 x 5/16. At the center, "as nearly as I can measure here," the sinew is 5/16 inches thick.

Glossary

Arm-guard — Same as *bracer*.

Arm — That part of an Asiatic composite bow lying between the siyah and the grip.

Back — Side of the bow away from the archer when in the act of shooting. Also back half of the bow-limb, measuring from the center line of the bow as in the composite.

Backing — A material such as sinew, rawhide, or canvas glued to the back of the bow to reduce breakage of bow-limbs and increase flexibility.

Belly — Side of the bow which faces the archer in the act of drawing.

Bowyer — One who makes bows.

Braced — When the bowstring is in the nocks and the bow is ready to be shot. Also spoken of as being "strung."

Bracer — A wrist guard which protects the wrist from the blow of the bowstring.

Bracing — The act of stringing the bow.

Cast — The maximum distance which a given bow will throw an arrow.

Cock-feather — The feather placed perpendicular to the notch in three-vane radial fletching; usually of a color differing from the other two.

Chest draw — A short draw. The bow arm held in front of the body with the draw to the chest.

Composite — A bow in which the proportions of horn belly to sinew back are approximately equal. In the true composite the limbs must also be reflexed. Often confused with "compound."

Compound — A bow made of two or more pieces of the same material. Often confused with "composite."

Cross chest draw — The Old English draw. Bow arm in line with shoulders and draw across chest; usually to the jaw.

D-bow — The simple bow.

Double-curved — A bow with deliberately deformed limbs; they first curve toward the back of the bow and then toward the belly.

Draw — The act of pulling the arrow back to shoot. Also the actual distance the arrow is pulled back in the bow measured from the front of the grip. Sometimes refers to the manner in which the drawing hand engages the arrow or the string in the act of pulling the arrow back.

Eye – The loop in the bowstring.

Fletching – The feathers used on an arrow. The act of applying feathers to an arrow. Also the manner in which it is done.

Following the string – The bend in a bow which is retained after the bow has been relaxed, caused by collapsing of wood cells on the belly side.

Footing – The front portion of a compound arrow of uniform diameter and normal length. The footing is usually attached to the shaft with a fish-tail splice and glue. Never seen in primitive arrows.

Foreshaft – A piece of hard wood inserted into the front end of an arrow or dart shaft. Originally served as the point or a means of holding a projectile point.

Guard – See *bracer*.

Horns – That portion of the bow beyond the nocks.

Knee – The junction between the siyah and the arm on an Asiatic composite.

Limbs – The bending portions of the bow; that part lying between the grip and the nocks.

Lining – Same as *backing*.

Lock – See *release*.

Nock – The notches cut in the horn of the bow to hold the bowstring. Also the extreme rear end of the arrow including the notch for the bowstring.

Noose – The knot at the lower end of the bowstring; usually a timber hitch.

Radial fletching – The normal way in which arrows are usually fletched. The vanes of the feather are used rather than the entire feather, and they are fastened perpendicular to the circumference of the shaft.

Recurved – Where the outer tips of the bow-limbs curve toward the back of the bow so that the bowstring actually contacts the belly side of the limb tips when the bow is braced. Never seen in primitive bows. Often confused with "reflexed."

Reflexed – Where the bow-limbs are set backward from the grip so higher stresses will be stored in the bow when brought to full draw. Often confused with "recurved."

Relaxed – The bow unstrung or unbraced.

Release – To let go the bowstring. Also the manner in which the arrow is drawn in the bow.

Rovers – A field game: shooting at objects chosen at random such as leaves, clods, etc. The winner of one shot chooses the next target.

Self-bow – A bow made of one piece of wood.

Shaftment – The portion of the arrow shaft bearing the fletching.

Sinew-backed — A bow with a backing of sinew.

Siyah — An Arabic word signifying "the stiff, unbending extremity of each limb" of the composite Asiatic bow.

Spine — The resistance of the arrow shaft to being bent; its stiffness.

Tangential fletching — The use of two or three whole feathers lashed flat to the shaftment of the arrow or dart.

Tillering — The art of securing uniform bending throughout the length of the limb. Usually achieved by bracing the bow, drawing repeatedly for inspection, and scraping down the stiff spots. Practiced only among advanced bowyers.

Thumb-ring — A ring worn by Oriental archers to protect the thumb from the bowstring when using the Mongolian draw or release.

Weight — The number of pounds pull exerted when a bow is drawn a given distance. The length of draw should always be stated when giving the weight of a bow.

Bibliography

Adler, Brune
1902

Die Bogen Nordasiens. INT. ARCHIV FUER ETH-NOGRAPHIE, Bd. 15, S. 1-27.

Balfour, Henry
1889

On the Structure and Affinities of the Composite Bow. JOURNAL OF THE ANTHROPOLOGICAL INSTI-TUTE, Vol. 19, pp 220-250.

Balfour, Henry
1897

On a Remarkable Ancient Bow and Arrows. JOUR-NAL OF THE ROYAL ANTHROPOLOGICAL INSTI-TUTE, Vol. 26, pp 210-220.

Barrington, Daines
1785

Observations on the Practice of Archery in England. ARCHAEOLOGIA, Vol. VII:46-68.

Belden, George P.
1875

BELDEN: THE WHITE CHIEF, or Twelve Years Among the Wild Indians of the Plains. Cincinnati.

Bendtsen, B.A.
1966

Letter addressed to T.M. Hamilton reporting on crush-ing strengths of elk antler, California yew and Moun-tain juniper.

Bradbury
1904

Bradbury's Travels in the Interior of America, 1809-1811. EARLY WESTERN TRAVELS, 1748-1846, Vol. V, Reuben Gold Thwaites, editor. The Arthur H. Clark Co. 1904.

Brereton, John
1602

Briefe and True Relation of the Discoverie of the North Part of Virginia, 1602. EARLY ENGLISH AND FRENCH VOYAGES, CHIEFLY FROM HAKLUYT, 1534-1608. Henry S. Burrage, editor, New York. 1906

Bridges
1949

THE UTTERMOST PARTS OF THE EARTH

Catlin, George
1857

ILLUSTRATIONS OF THE MANNERS, CUSTOMS, AND CONDITION OF THE AMERICAN INDIANS, London.

Chard, Chester S.
1958

An Outline of the Prehistory of Siberia, Part I. The Pre-Metal Periods. S.W. JOURNAL OF ANTHROPOL-OGY, Vol. 14, #1.

Clark, J.G.D.
1963

Neolithic Bows from Somerset, England, and the Prehistory of Archery in Northwestern Europe. PROCEEDINGS OF THE PREHISTORIC SOCIETY, Vol. XXIX, pp 50-98.

Clark, Wm.P.
1884

THE INDIAN SIGN LANGUAGE

Cosgrove, C.B.
1947

Caves of the Upper Gila and Hueco Areas in New Mexico and Texas. PAPERS OF THE PEABODY MUSEUM OF AMERICAN ARCHAEOLOGY AND ETHNOLOGY. XXIV, 2, Cambridge.

Currelly, C.T.
1939

The Weight of an Arrow. AMERICAN ANTIQUITY, IV, 4, p 351.

Elvas
1907

The Narrative of the Expedition of Hernando De Soto, by the Gentleman of Elvas. SPANISH EXPLORATIONS IN THE SOUTHERN UNITED STATES, 1528-1543. [Original Narratives of Early American History, Scribner's, 1907.]

Evans, Clifford and
Betty Meggers
1957

Letter to T.M. Hamilton on Wai Wai archery.

Faris and Elmer
1945

ARAB ARCHERY, Princeton University Press.

Fenenga, Franklin
1953

The Weights of Chipped Stone Points; A Clue to Their Functions. SOUTHWESTERN JOURNAL OF ANTHROPOLOGY, 9, 3, pp 309-323.

Galvez, Bernardo de
1786

INSTRUCTIONS FOR GOVERNING THE INTERIOR PROVINCES OF NEW SPAIN, 1786. Translated and edited by Donald E. Worcester, The Quivira Society, Berkeley, 1951.

Garcilaso De La Vega
1951

FLORIDA OF THE INCA, Translated by John Grier Varner and Jeannette Johnson Varner, University of Texas Press.

Gilbert, Captain
1906

Relation of a Voyage to Sagadahoc, 1607-1608. EARLY ENGLISH AND FRENCH VOYAGES, CHIEFLY FROM HAKLUYT, 1534-1608. Henry S. Burrage, editor. Original Narratives of Early American History, Scribner's, 1906.

Guernsey, Samuel James
1931

Explorations in Northeastern Arizona. PAPERS OF PEABODY MUSEUM OF AMERICAN ARCHAEOLOGY AND ETHNOLOGY, XII, 1.

Guernsey, Samuel and Kidder, A.V.
1921
Basket-Maker Caves of Northeastern Arizona. PEABODY MUSEUM OF AMERICAN ARCHAEOLOGY AND ETHNOLOGY, VIII, 2.

Hamilton, Henry W.
1952
The Spiro Mound. THE MISSOURI ARCHAEOLOGIST, Vol. 14.

Hammond, George P. and Rey, Agapito
1929
EXPEDITION INTO NEW MEXICO MADE BY ANTONIO DE ESPEJO, 1582-1583, as revealed in the Journal of Diego Perez de Luxan.

———
1953
DON JUAN DE ONATE, COLONIZER OF NEW MEXICO, 1595-1628.

Hansard, George Agar
1841
THE BOOK OF ARCHERY. London.

Harrington, Mark R.
1933
Gypsum Cave, Nevada. SOUTHWEST MUSEUM PAPERS, #8. Los Angeles.

Hawkins, M. John
1906
The Voyage Made by M. John Hawkins, Esq., 1565. EARLY ENGLISH AND FRENCH VOYAGES, 1534-1608. Henry S. Burrage, editor. Scribner's, 1906.

———
1906
The Third Voyage, by M. John Hawkins, 1567-1568. EARLY ENGLISH AND FRENCH VOYAGES, 1534-1608. Henry S. Burrage, editor. Scribner's, 1906.

Hein, Joachim
1925-26
Bogenhandwerk und Bogensport bei den Osmanen. DER ISLAM, Bd. 14, S.289-360; 15, S.1-78.

Heizer, Robert F.
1938
A complete Atlatl Dart from Pershing County, Nevada. NEW MEXICO ANTHROPOLOGIST, II, 4 & 5, pp 70-1.

———
1953
Additional Notes on Chinese Soapstone Carvings From Meso-America. AMERICAN ANTIQUITY, Vol. XIX, #1, p 81.

Henry and Thompson
1897
NEW LIGHT ON THE EARLY HISTORY OF THE GREAT NORTHWEST. Edited by Elliott Coues. New York.

Hill, Malcolm W.
1948
A recent Study of Atlatls in Use with Darts of Various Sizes. TENNESSEE ARCHAEOLOGIST, IV, 4, pp 37-44.

Holmberg, Allan R.
1950
NOMADS OF THE LONG BOW. Smithsonian Institution, Institute of Social Anthropology, Pub. #10.

Jenness, Diamond
1922
The Life of Copper Eskimos. REPORT OF THE CANADIAN ARTIC EXPEDITION, 1913-18, Vol. XII.

———   *Material Culture of the Copper Eskimo.* REPORT OF
1946   THE CANADIAN ARCTIC EXPEDITION,
     1913–1918, Vol. XVI.

Kellar, James H.   *The Atlatl in North America.* PREHISTORY RE-
1955   SEARCH SERIES, III, 3. Indiana Historical Society,
     Indianapolis.

Kelley, J. Charles   *Atlatls, Bows and Arrows, Pictographs, and the Pecos*
1950   *River Focus.* AMERICAN ANTIQUITY, XVI, 1.

Kidder, A.V.   *Arrow-Heads or Dart Points?* AMERICAN ANTIQ-
1938   UITY, IV, 2, pp 156-157.

Kidder, A.V. and   ARCHAEOLOGICAL EXPLORATIONS IN NORTH-
Guernsey, Samuel J.   EASTERN ARIZONA. Bureau of American Ethnol-
1919   ogy, Bul. 65.

Klopsteg, Paul E.   TURKISH ARCHERY AND THE COMPOSITE BOW.
1947   Evanston, Illinois.

———   *Bows and Arrows: A Chapter in the Evolution of*
1963   *Archery in America.* SMITHSONIAN ANNUAL RE-
     PORT FOR 1962, pp 567-592.

Koeppen, Robert C.   Undated note to Dale Henning identifying wood in
N.D.   various Indian bows.

———   Letter addressed to T.M. Hamilton reporting crushing
1965   strength of various bowwoods.

Kurz, Rudolph Friederich   Journal Friederich Kurz. Bul. 115, American Bureau of
1937   Ethnology.

Laudonniere, Rene   *The Second Voyage unto Florida, made and written by*
1907   *Captaine Laudonniere, which fortified and inhabited*
     there two Summers and one Whole Winter. HAK-
     LUYT'S VOYAGES, Vol. XI. Everyman's Library.

La Flesche, Francis   *Omaha Bow and Arrow Makers.* SMITHSONIAN AN-
1926   NUAL REPORT, 1926, pp 487-94.

Leeper, D.R.   *Survivals of the Stone Age.* THE ANTIQUARIAN, Vol.
1897   1, # 8: 197-202. Columbus, Ohio.

Loud, Llewellyn L. and   *Lovelock Cave.* UNIVERSITY OF CALIFORNIA PUB-
Harrington, Mark R.   LICATIONS IN AMERICAN ARCHAEOLOGY AND
1929   ETHNOLOGY, XXV, 1.

Longman, C.J.   *The Bows of the Ancient Assyrians and Egyptians.*
1894   JOURNAL OF THE ROYAL ANTHROPOLOGICAL
     INSTITUTE, Vol. 24, pp 49-57.

Longman and Walrond 1894	ARCHERY. Reprinted 1967 by Fredrick Ungar Co.
Lorant, Stefan 1946	THE NEW WORLD. Duell, Sloan and Pearce.
Lowie, Robert H. 1924	*Notes on Shoshonean Ethnography.* ANTHROPOLOGICAL PAPERS OF THE AMERICAN MUSEUM OF NATURAL HISTORY, XX, III. New York.
Luschan, Felix von 1893	*Einen Zusammengesetzten Bogen aus der Zeit Rhamses II.* ZEITSCHRIFT FUER ETHNOLOGIE, Bd. XXV, S.266-271.
————————	*Zusammengesetzte und Verstaerkte Bogen.* ZEITSCHRIFT FUER ETHNOLOGIE, Bd. XXXI, S.221-239.
Mason, Otis T. 1886	*The Ray Collection from Hupa Reservation.* SMITHSONIAN ANNUAL REPORT, 1886, Pt. I. pp 225-230.
———————— 1893	*North American Bows, Arrows and Quivers.* SMITHSONIAN ANNUAL REPORT, 1893. pp 631-681.
McLeod, Wallace E.	An unpublished Egyptian Composite Bow in the Brooklyn Museum. AMERICAN JOURNAL OF ARCHAEOLOGY, Vol. 62, pp 397-401, Plates 108 & 109.
———————— 1962	*Egyptian Composite Bows in New York.* AMERICAN JOURNAL OF ARCHAEOLOGY, Vol. 66, pp 13-19, Plates 11 & 12.
Metcalf, George 1957	A detailed description accompanying his letter of ten horn bows now in the U.S. National Museum.
Metraux, Alfred 1945	HANDBOOK OF THE SOUTH AMERICAN INDIANS, V. Bureau of American Ethnology Bulletin 143.
Meyer, Hermann 1896	*Bows and Arrows in Central Brazil.* SMITHSONIAN ANNUAL REPORT.
Miller, Alfred Jacob 1951	THE WEST OF ALFRED JACOB MILLER (edited by Marvin C. Ross), University of Oklahoma Press.
Morse, Edward S. 1885	*Ancient and Modern Methods of Arrow Release.* BULLETIN OF THE ESSEX INSTITUTE, XVII, Oct.-Dec. Salem, Massachusetts.
———————— 1888	ADDITIONAL NOTES ON ARROW RELEASES. Peabody Museum, Salem, Massachusetts.

Murdoch, John
1884

A study of Eskimo Bows in the U.S. National Museum.
SMITHSONIAN ANNUAL REPORT, 1884. pp
307-316.

Nelson, Edward William
1899

THE ESKIMO ABOUT BERING STRAIT. 18th Annual Report of the Bureau of American Ethnology.

Nuttal, Z.
1910

The Island of Sacrificios. AMERICAN ANTHROPOLOGIST, Vol. 12, pp 256-295.

Percy, George
1907

Observations of Master George Percy, 1607. NARRATIVES OF EARLY VIRGINIA, 1606-1625. Lyon
Gardiner Tyler, editor. Scribner's, 1907.

Pope, Saxton
1918

Yahi Archery. UNIVERSITY OF CALIFORNIA PUBLICATIONS IN AMERICAN ARCHAEOLOGY AND
ETHNOLOGY, 13, 3.

⸻
1923

A study in Bows and Arrows. UNIVERSITY OF
CALIFORNIA PUBLICATIONS IN AMERICAN
ARCHAEOLOGY AND ETHNOLOGY, 13, 9.

Powell, J.W.
1875

EXPLORATION OF THE COLORADO RIVER OF
THE WEST AND ITS TRIBUTARIES. Smithsonian
Institution.

Pring, Martin
1906

A Voyage Set Out from the Citie of Bristoll, 1603.
EARLY ENGLISH AND FRENCH VOYAGES CHIEFLY FROM HAKLUYT. Henry S. Burrage, editor.
Scribner's, New York, 1906.

Rausing, Gad
1967

THE BOW: SOME NOTES ON ITS ORIGIN AND
DEVELOPMENT. Gleerups, Lund, Sweden.

Rogers, Spencer L.
1940

*The Aboriginal Bow and Arrow in North America and
Eastern Asia.* AMERICAN ANTHROPOLOGIST, Vol.
42, #2.

Rosier, James
1906

A True Relation of Captain George Waumouth, his
Voyage, made this present yeere 1605. EARLY ENGLISH AND FRENCH VOYAGES CHIEFLY FROM
HAKLUYT. Henry S. Burrage, editor. Scribner's, 1906.

Roth, Walter Edmund
1916

An Introductory Study of the Arts, Crafts and Customs of the Guiana Indians. 36th ANNUAL REPORT,
Bureau of American Ethnology.

Schroeder, Albert H.
1963

Letters addressed to T.M. Hamilton concerning early
Spanish references to the "Turkish" bow encountered
along the Rio Grande.

Smith, Capt. John
1907

A map of Virginia: With a description of the Countrey, etc. NARRATIVES OF EARLY VIRGINIA, 1606-1625. Edited by Lyon Gardiner Tyler. Scribner's, New York, 1907.

—————————
1907

A True Relation. NARRATIVES OF EARLY VIRGINIA, 1606-1625. Edited by Lyon Gardiner Tyler. Scribner's, New York, 1907.

Spier, Leslie
1928

Havasupai Ethnography. ANTHROPOLOGICAL PAPERS OF THE AMERICAN MUSEUM OF NATURAL HISTORY, 29, #3.

Swanton, John R.
1911

Indian Tribes of the Lower Mississippi Valley, Bulletin 43, Bureau of American Ethnology.

Teit, James A.

Salishan Tribes of the Plateaus. 45th ANNUAL REPORT, Bureau of American Ethnology.

Thompson, David
1916

DAVID THOMPSON'S NARRATIVE OF HIS EXPLORATIONS IN WESTERN AMERICA. Toronto.

Tixier, Victor
1940

TRAVELS ON THE OSAGE PRAIRIES. Edited by John Francis McDermott, translated by Albert Barnaby. University of Oklahoma Press.

de Vaca, Cabeza
1907

The Narrative of Cabeza de Vaca. SPANISH EXPLORERS IN THE SOUTHERN UNITED STATES. Original Narratives of Early American History. Scribner's, New York.

Webb, Clarence H. and Ralph R. McKinney
1963

An Unusual Pottery Vessel from the Mounds Plantation Site, Caddo Parish, Louisiana. ARKANSAS ARCHAEOLOGIST, Vol. IV, #5.

Webb, Clarence H.
1967

Letter to T.M. Hamilton dated April 9, 1967.

White, Father Andrew
1943

A Brief Relation of a Voyage Unto Maryland, 1639. NARRATIVES OF EARLY MARYLAND, Phelps, 1943.

White, John
1907

The Fourth Voyage Made to Virginia in the Yere 1587. EARLY ENGLISH AND FRENCH VOYAGES CHIEFLY FROM HAKLUYT, 1534-1608. Edited by Henry S. Burrage. Scribner's, New York, 1907.

Wilson, E.N.
1919

THE WHITE INDIAN BOY. Revised and edited by Howard R. Driggs. Yonkers-on-Hudson.

Wilson, Gilbert L.
MS

Unpublished manuscript on the material culture of the Hidatsa. American Museum of Natural History.

Wissler, Clark
1910

Material Culture of the Blackfoot Indians. ANTHRO-POLOGICAL PAPERS OF THE AMERICAN MUSE-UM OF NATURAL HISTORY, Vol. 5.

Zahn, F.B.
1956

Letter to T.M. Hamilton.

——————————
1957

Letter to T.M. Hamilton.

Index

89; type description, 90; ratio of horn to sinew, 106; unconfirmed among the Osage, 109

composite, Asiatic, early speculation on origin, 70; flight record, 71; general description, 71; action of siyahs, 78; various hypotheses on origin, 85

coup counting with bow, 108

crushing strength, 60

Custer fight, 108

D

Dakotah bow, description of a, 58

dart, Garcilasco's description, 12; typical, 14; fletching of, 15; foreshaft, 15, 16; Pershing County dart described, 16; Gypsum Cave, 17

dart point vs. arrowhead, distinction between, 26

D-bow, defined, 6; possible Eskimo prototype, 75; best Eskimo design, 83

double-curved bow, defined, 6; a peculiar fad, 46; possible reason for, 48; confused with reinforced, 59; as reinforced bow, 103; used by Sioux, 108

Drake, Sir Francis, on Indian archery, 67

draw, 1; limits to length of, 2; of Osage bow, 41; reduced by shorter bow, 44; of Siriono bow, 49; of reinforced bow, 66; of Eskimo bow, 83; of elkhorn bows, 98

E

ears, see siyahs

Egyptian bows, 87

Elder, R. A., Jr., 104

elkhorn bow, Neolithic bowstaves found at Lake Baikal, 75; used by native American bowmakers, 86; type description, 90; described by Alfred Jacob Miller, 90; Wolf-chief's comments on, 96; crushing strength of elkhorn, 98

English, archers, 32, 33; flight shots, 97

Eskimo bow, general description, 75; types described, 82; tested by Pope, 83; derived from Asiatic composite, 83; genesis of, 85

Evans, Clifford, and Betty Meggers, observations of Wai-Wai archery, 48

F

Faris and Elmer, ARAB ARCHERY, 92

feathers, see fletching

Finsbury Field, plan of, 36

Flathead, description of bow, 105

fletching, tangential, 16; radial, 16; Gypsum cave dart, 17; Martin Pring on, 22; Plains arrows, 22; Roth's types, 22; examples found in caves, 24; Wai-Wai, 56; Ona, 57

flight records, with composite, 70: Ford's using longbow, 97

foreshaft, use on the dart, 14; as a structural convenience, 17; functional vs. non-functional, 21; on arrows from cave, 24; on Wai-Wai and Colombian arrows, 54

Ford, H. A., flight record by, 97

Four-horn's feat, 109

free sinew back, 85

G

Galvez, Bernardo De, on desirability of arming Indians with guns, 112

Garcilasco de la Vega, on atlatl and dart, 12

glue, possible only after invention of pottery, 75; made from salmon skins, 93; used on splice in handle, 94

Great Basin, 41

Guernsey, Samuel J., 41

gun, quickly supplants the bow east of Mississippi, 29; completely changes hunting complex, 29

H

Hale, Willie, describes how his father made elkhorn bows, 96
Hansard, George Agar, 107
Hawkins, John, describes bows of Florida, 39
Hein, Joachim, describes bows of California, 71
Henry and Thompson, on Plains bows before advent of the horse, 92, 97
Hidatsa bow-making described by Wilson, 94
Holmberg, Allan R., on Siriono archery, 49
horn, requirements for composite bow, 92; its use in the belly, 92; hypothesis of its function, 103
horn bow, see composite, American
horse bow, 44
Hunkpapa archery, 107
Hupa, making of bow, 68; cast of bow, 69

I

Ishi, used juniper for bow, 61; tests bows, 68

J

Jenness, Diamond, 83
Juniper, Rocky Mountain, crushing strength, 60; used on both types of reinforced bows, 61

K

Kani, Mustafa, 71
knees, 78
knots, 61
Keoppen, Robert C., on crushing strengths, 98
Kurz, Rudolph Friederich, 92
Lake Baikal, antler "laths" from, 75; possible significance of "laths," 87

L

lemonwood, the use of, 49
lining, see sinew lined or backed bows
Le Moyne, 36, 46
locust, black, crushing strength, 60
Longman, C. J., 87
loop, 69
Lowie, Robert H., 92
Luschan, Felix von, 70, 71, 85, 87

M

marksmanship, exaggeration in early accounts, 107; Sioux, 109; Osage, 109; Snake, 112
McLeod, Wallace E., on Egyptian composites, 87
Metcalf, George, search for pre-contact evidence of horn bow, 92; assists in finding Flathead bow, 104; on dimensions of Flathead bow, 105
Mexico, southern limit of reinforced bow, 48
Miller, Alfred Jacob, comments on the elkhorn bow, 97; his paintings, 98; on Snake marksmanship, 112
mountain sheep horn, see bighorn
Murdoch, John, his classification of Eskimo bows, 87
muzzle-loaders, Sioux opinion of, 108, 112

N

National Wood Products Laboratory, 98
Nelson, Edward William, 83
nocks, Rosier's observations on East Coast, 33; on Plains bows, 46; as normally found on reinforced bows, 59; how bowstring was attached to elkhorn bows, 94; on Sioux bows, 108
noose in place of loop, 95
notches, see nocks

O

oak, white, crushing strength, 60

Okladnikov, A. P., discovers antler laths at Lake Baikal, 75; possible importance of discovery, 87

Omaha bow-making, 44

Ona archery, 56

Osage orange, best bow-wood, 4; Indian bow described, 41; a bow of presumed Indian _manufacture described, 47; crushing strength, 60; Bradbury's comments on, 97; unknown to Sioux, 108

P

pampas, Indians did not adapt bow to the horse, 57

Percy, George, tests East Coast bow, 33

Piegan evaluation of horn bow, 97

Pitt-Rivers, General, on the Asiatic composite, 71

Plains Indians, modified bow to horse, 57, develop the horn bow, 75; as archers, 107

Pope, Saxton, makes replica of the Sudbury bow, 32; reports bow-wood used by Ishi, 61; tests Eskimo bow, 83

Powell, John. W., 92

Pueblo bows found by Guernsey, 41

R

ram's horn, see bighorn

Rausing, Gad, importance of pottery in making glue, 75

reflex, defined, 9; a feature of the reinforced bow, 58; on Apache bow, 58; confused with the double-curved, 59; why reinforced bows may appear to be double-curved, 59; Ray's comments, 68; greater in Asiatic composite horn bows, 71; in the Flathead bow, 105

reinforced bow, defined, 6, 58; theory of, 61; distribution of, 62; making of, 62; performance of, 64; the "Turkish bow," 65; power of, 66; draw and weight, 66; deformation of bow-limbs, 103

release, power of the Tertiary, 110

reversed in the string, 59

Rio Grande, 48

Rosier, James, comments on East Coast bows, 33

S

Schuyler, Remington, comments on Plains Indian shooting, 110

self-bow, defined, 2; distribution of, 29; toy, 30; Sudbury bow, 30; early English, 32; comments by Father Andrew White, 33; comment by George Percy, 33; comment by James Rosier, 33; pictures by White, 33, 39; Mounds Plantation bow, 36; pictures by De Bry, 36; pictures by Le Moyne, 36; comment by Laudonniere, 39; Osage orange, 41; Pueblo, 41; comment by David Thompson, 42; Spiro mound, 42; La Flesche, Francis, 44; Siriono, 48; Wai-Wai, 54

Shakespeare, William, on flight shooting, 97

Sharp-horn-bull, killing a steer, 108; skill at the "game of the arrow," 109; hitting a moccasin in air, 109; his draw and release, 110

Shoshone, 98

sinew, 93, 94, 102

sinew cable back, see free sinew back

sinew lined or backed bow, see reinforced bow

sinew lining (or backing), 68, 83, 106

Sioux archery, 107-109

siyahs (or ears), 70, 82, 83, 87; function of, 78

slack-string bow defined, 6

Smithsonian Institution, 104

snakeskin, as a cover for composites, 103, 108
South America, 48
Southwest, 41
splice, in elkhorn bow, 94; in bighorn bow, 95; in buffalo rib bow, 102
Spotted Bear, 110; interview with, 102, 109
Spiro mound bows, 42
stalking game, 29
Sudbury bow, 30

T

Teit, James A., on the horn bow, 93
tensile stress, 89
Terra del Fuego, 48, 56
Thompson, David, describes early Plain bows, 42
tillering, defined, 5; in the Sudbury bow, 32; absence in Omaha bows, 46, the horn bow, 86
"Turkish bows" of the Southwest, 65

U

U. S. National Museum, 104

W

Washo, arrow and bow, 69
weight, defined, 1; in self-bows, 31; 41; 52, 57; in reinforced bows, 66; in Eskimo bow, 83
western bows, more information on, 41
White, Andrew, 33
White, John, 33
Wilson, Gilbert L., 94, 96
Wilson, E. N., 92
Wissler, Clark, 59
Wolf-chief on making horn bows, 94-96

Y

Yana bows, 69
Yanktonai shooting, 107
Yew, Pacific, crushing strength, 60
Yurok bows, 69

Z

Zahn, F. B., letters from, 102, 107

The Author

T. M. Hamilton, here shown holding a double-curved bow, is a specialist on frontier weapons. He is best known by archaeologists for his work with gunflints and gun fragments recovered from historic sites, and he is the acknowledged authority on the identification and dating of guns and gun parts found in 17th and 18th Century contexts.

His investigation of native American bows began with a gift of a Plains bow from his brother, Henry W. Hamilton. In this book Mr. Hamilton summarizes twenty-seven years of intermittent research on the problem of how well the natives understood the basic theories of bow construction and how well their products shot. He and Mrs. Hamilton have visited most of the important museums in the Eastern United States, examining the bows in the storerooms as well as those on display. The result is the first comprehensive discussion of the various bow types developed in the Western Hemisphere and their interrelationships.

The Hamilton home in central Missouri is on a high bluff above the Missouri River. The study window overlooks the crossing point of an important Indian trail in the old days. About five miles away lies the fabulous Utz site, over a hundred acres in extent, where the Missouri Indians had their village for generations, and where the University of Missouri now maintains the Lyman Center for Archaeological Research and the Hamilton Field School. The field school is named in honor of the Hamilton brothers and their wives in recognition of their services to Missouri archaeology.

Mr. Hamilton feels that he has worked out a rather satisfactory compromise with life. He spends his summers farming in partnership with his brother Henry and son George. His winters are spent in research and writing.

Other Writings by T. M. Hamilton

1953   *Archaeological Photography.* MISSOURI ARCHAEOLOGIST, Vol. 15, #1 & 2. pp 42-76.

1956   *A Black Sand Site in Saline County, Missouri.* MISSOURI ARCHAEOL-OGIST, Vol. 18, #4. pp 34-48.

1960   *Indian Trade Guns.* (T.M. Hamilton, compiler) MISSOURI ARCHAE-OLOGIST, Vol. 22 (Whole volume), viii plus 223 pp. Contains following contributions by T.M. Hamilton:

> *The Determination of Date and Origin of Archaeological Gun Parts.* pp 5-15.
> *Additional Comments on Gunflints.* pp 73-79.
> *Some Gun Parts from 17th Century Seneca Sites.* pp 99-108.
> *Some Gun Parts from 18th Century Osage Sites.* pp 120-149.
> *The Gunsmith's Cache Discovered at Malta Bend, Missouri.* pp 150-171.
> *Concluding Comments and Observations.* pp 207-209.
> Appendix. pp 211-218.

1964   *Recent Developments in the Use of Gunflints for Dating and Identification.* DIVING INTO THE PAST. (Holmquist and Wheeler, Editors) pp 52-57. Minnesota Historical Society, St. Paul.

1965   *18th Century Gun Cache Uncovered!* THE GUN DIGEST, 1965. pp 138-139.

1968a   Review of *A History of Gunflints* by John Witthoft. HISTORICAL ARCHAEOLOGY 1968.

1968b   EARLY INDIAN TRADE GUNS, 1625-1775. ix plus 34 pp, 20 plates. Museum of the Great Plains, Lawton, Oklahoma.

1969   *A Cree Bow with Sinew Backing; Its possible relationship to bows of the Arctic and the High Plains.* THE MUSEUM OF THE FUR TRADE QUARTERLY, Vol. 5, #3. pp 4-8.

1969   The Gunflints of Sept-Iles and Mingan.
THE CONFERENCE ON HISTORIC SITE ARCHAEOLOGY
PAPERS, 1969. Stanley South, Editor. Columbia, S.C.

1970   Making the Flight Arrow.
(Translation from Joachim Hein's *Bogenhandwerk und Bogensport bei den Osmannen.*)
JOURNAL OF THE SOCIETY OF ARCHER ANTIQUARIES, Vol. 13.

1970   The Eskimo Bow and the Asiatic Composite.
ARTIC ANTHROPOLOGY, Vol. vl, #2. pp 43-52.

1975   A Survey of Louisbourg Gunflints.
CANADIAN HISTORIC SITES, No. 12.
(With Bruce Fry)

1975   L'arc Renforce des Hautes Plaines D'amerique.
GAZETTE DES ARMES, No. 25. March 1975
Paris

MS   The Rhodes Site Guns.
To be published by the Illinois State Museum in their report on the Rhodes Site.

1976   FIREARMS ON THE FRONTIER: Guns at Fort Michilimackinac.
Reports in Mackinac History and Archaeology, No. 5 Mackinac Island State Park Commission.

1976   Concerning the Construction of the Crossbow in the Late Middle Ages.
(Translation of Fritz Rohde's *Ueber die Zusammensetzung der Spaetmittelalterlichen Armburst)* JOURNAL OF THE SOCIETY OF ARCHER ANTIQUARIES, Vol. 19.

1977   L.' Armurier des Frontieres a L'Epoque Coloniale.
GAZETTE DES ARMES, No. 52: 32-27.

1980   COLONIAL FRONTIER GUNS. 176 pp, 97 figures.
The Fur Press, Chadron, Nebraska.

1980   Guns, gunflints, balls and shot.
In TUNICA TREASURE by Jeffry P. Brain.
Peabody Museum, Harvard. pp. 206 to 216.